"This is a poignant and compelling memoir about the impact of bipolar disorder on one person's life. The writing is outstanding; the story is gripping. Ms. Cheney reveals the multiple facets—psychological, physiological, and existential—of living with this illness. The descriptions of the many aspects of bipolar disorder, including depression, hypomania, mania, and mixed states, are portrayed in extraordinary detail. This book is a must-read for all those, clinicians and laypersons alike, who are interested in deeply understanding the experience of having bipolar disorder."

—Dr. Lori Altshuler, Director
of the UCLA Mood Disorders Research Program

"Cheney . . . writes with passionate clarity about depression and the lure of suicide, but with especially keen intensity about mania."   —Boston Globe

"Superb. . . . Cheney's remarkable chronicle of her painful odyssey is as eloquent as it is brave. It is also profoundly necessary, both for her and for us."   —Providence Journal

MANIC

Terri Cheney

MANIC

a memoir

HARPER

NEW YORK • LONDON • TORONTO • SYDNEY

HARPER

A hardcover edition of this book was published in 2008 by William Morrow, an imprint of HarperCollins Publishers.

FIRST HARPER PAPERBACK PUBLISHED 2009.

Designed by Kate Nichols

Library of Congress Cataloging-in-Publication Data has been applied for.

ISBN 978-0-06-143027-5

23 24 25 26 27 LBC 23 22 21 20 19

To my mother and father

MANIC

Preface

If you come with me on this journey, I think
a word of warning is in order: manic depression is not a safe
ride. It doesn't go from point A to point B in a familiar, friendly
pattern. It's chaotic, unpredictable. You never know where
you're heading next. I wanted this book to mirror the disease,
to give the reader a visceral experience. That's why I've
chosen to tell my life story episodically, rather than in any
chronological order. It's truer to the way I think. When I look
back, I rarely remember events in terms of date or sequence.
Rather, I remember what emotional state I was in. Manic?
Depressed? Suicidal? Euphoric? Life for me is defined not by
time, but by mood.

I've tried to stay as true as I can to what I remember. But mental illness creates its own vibrant reality, which is so convincing it's sometimes hard to figure out exactly what is real and what is not. It gets even harder as time goes by, because memory is the first casualty of manic depression. When I'm manic, all I remember is the moment. When I'm depressed, all I remember is the pain. The surrounding details are lost on me.

But the illness, ironically, has impaired me far less than the treatment. I've long since lost track of all the psychotropic medications I've had to take over the years, or the nature and number of their side effects. More devastating, however, was the course of electroshock therapy (ECT) I went through in 1994. ECT can be of great help as a last-resort treatment, but it's notorious for wiping out memory. For a while, I forgot even the simplest things: what part of town I lived in, my mother's maiden name, what scissors were for. Some of this was eventually restored, but I still have trouble recalling past events and retaining the memories of new ones. The world has never seemed as sharp and clear as it did before the ECT.

In some cases, the events I describe can be documented by police or hospital records (although some of the hospitals no longer exist). I've elected to change the names of most of the people and institutions depicted, to protect their identities. The experiences I've written about are often difficult and private, and I prefer just to tell my own story.

Telling my story is what's kept me alive, even when death was at its most seductive. That's why I've chosen to share my personal history, although some of it is still painful to recall even through a haze of medication, mental illness, and electroshock therapy. But the disease thrives on shame, and shame thrives on silence, and I've been silent long enough. This book represents what I remember. This book is my truth.

Terri Cheney
Los Angeles, California

I

I didn't tell anyone that I was going to Santa Fe

to kill myself. I figured that was more information than

people needed, plus it might interfere with my travel plans

if anyone found out the truth. People always mean well, but

they don't understand that when you're seriously depressed,

suicidal ideation can be the only thing that keeps you alive.

Just knowing there's an out—even if it's bloody, even if it's

permanent—makes the pain almost bearable for one more day.

Five months had passed since my father's death from lung

cancer, and the world was not a fit place to live in. As long as

Daddy was still alive, it made sense to get up every morning,

depressed or not. There was a war on. But the day I gave the order to titrate his morphine to a lethal dose, the fight lost all meaning for me.

So I wanted to die. I saw nothing odd about this desire, even though I was only thirty-eight years old. It seemed like a perfectly natural response, under the circumstances. I was bone-tired, terminally weary, and death sounded like a vacation to me, a holiday. A somewhere else, which is all I really wanted.

When I was offered the chance to leave L.A. to take an extended trip by myself to Santa Fe, I was ecstatic. I leased a charming little hacienda just off Canyon Road, the artsiest part of town, bursting with galleries, jazz clubs, and eccentric, cat-ridden bookstore/cafés. It was a good place to live, especially in December, when the snow fell thick and deep on the cobblestones, muffling the street noise so thoroughly that the city seemed to dance its own soft-shoe.

There was an exceptional amount of snowfall that particular December. Everything seemed a study in contrast: the fierce round desert sun, blazing while I shivered; blue-white snow shadows against thick red adobe walls; and always, everywhere I looked, the sagging spine of the old city pressing up against the sleek curves of the new. But the most striking contrast by far was me: thrilled to tears simply to be alive in such surroundings, and determined as ever to die.

I never felt so bipolar in my life.

The mania came at me in four-day spurts. Four days of not eating, not sleeping, barely sitting in one place for more than a few minutes at a time. Four days of constant shopping—and Canyon Road is all about commerce, however artsy its facade. And four days of indiscriminate, nonstop talking: first to everyone I knew on the West Coast, then to anyone still awake on the East Coast, then to Santa Fe itself, whoever would listen. The truth was, I didn't just need to talk. I was afraid to be alone. There were things hovering in the air around me that didn't want to be remembered: the expression on my father's face when I told him it was stage IV cancer, already metastasized; the bewildered look in his eyes when I couldn't take away the pain; and the way those eyes kept watching me at the end, trailing my every move, fixed on me, begging for the comfort I wasn't able to give. I never thought I could be haunted by anything so familiar, so beloved, as my father's eyes.

Mostly, however, I talked to men. Canyon Road has a number of extremely lively, extremely friendly bars and clubs, all of which were within walking distance of my hacienda. It wasn't hard for a redhead with a ready smile and a feverish glow in her eyes to strike up a conversation and then continue that conversation well into the early-morning hours, at his place or mine. The only word I couldn't seem to say was "no." I ease my conscience by reminding myself that manic sex isn't really intercourse. It's discourse, just another way to ease the insatiable need for contact and communication. In place of words, I simply spoke with my skin.

I had long since decided that Christmas Eve would be my last day on this earth. I chose Christmas Eve precisely because it had meaning and beauty—nowhere more so than in Santa

Fe, with its enchanting festival of the *farolitos*. Every Christmas Eve, carolers come from all over the world to stroll the lantern-lit streets until dawn. All doors are open to them, and the air is pungent with the smell of warm cider and piñon.

I wanted to die at such a moment, when the world was at its best, when I could offer up my heart to God and say, thank you, truly, for all of it. It's not that I'm ungrateful. It's just that I'm not capable anymore of the joy a night like this deserves. Joy is blasphemy now that Daddy's dead; your world is simply wasted on me. And that, I think, is reason enough to die. This unwritten prayer was the only suicide note I intended to leave.

Christmas Eve dawned bright and cold, with snow in the forecast for early that afternoon. I was on the fourth day of my latest manic spree, which meant my mind was speeding so fast I had to make shorthand lists to keep up with it. I'd already carefully laid out what I was going to wear as my farewell attire: a long black cashmere dress—not to be macabre, but because cashmere would never wrinkle and black would hide any unexpected blood or vomit. I'd also laid out all the pills I'd saved up over the past year, including all the heavy-duty cancer meds my father had never lived long enough to take. They were neatly arranged in probable order of lethality, and grouped into manageable mouthfuls, approximately ten pills per swallow. Counting them one last time, I realized I had well over three hundred assorted tablets and capsules, which meant an awful lot of swallows. What I didn't have was sufficient tequila to wash them all down. Water wasn't an option. I needed the interaction.

So it couldn't be helped. I pulled on my gloves, hat, and coat, grabbed my car keys off the counter, and dashed off to the nearest liquor store, praying it was open. The snow was falling just heavily enough to slow my progress, but I was in luck. Not only were they still open, but my favorite tequila, Lapiz in the cobalt blue bottle, was on sale. I bought a fifth, then turned around and bought two more. There seemed little point, after all, in economizing. The old sales clerk, who had waited on me many times that December, held out his hand and wished me a merry Christmas. I shook his hand briefly, then turned back and gave him a big hug and a kiss on both cheeks. "Merry Christmas," I said, as something cold and sharp twanged inside me. I had promised myself no good-byes.

The snow was falling thick and fast by the time I got back to the hacienda. The car heater wasn't working very well, and I was shivering so hard I could barely open my purse to get the house key. I hated being cold. Rummaging through my purse with half-numb fingers, I wondered if the body felt the grave, and if that final chill ever truly left the bones. Five frustrating minutes later, I realized the key wasn't anywhere in my purse, nor was it in the car, nor was it lying outside in the snow. It was, quite simply, somewhere else; and I was locked out of my most desperate dream.

Fortunately, my cell phone was in the glove compartment, charged and ready. A helpful operator took pity on me and managed to find me the only local locksmith working on Christmas Eve. But it would be at least an hour, the locksmith told me, before he could make it over to Canyon Road. "Better bundle up and stay warm," he said. "I'll do better than that,"

I thought. Uncorking the bottle of Lapiz, I took a long, deep swallow, and started singing Christmas carols alphabetically to myself.

I'd been around the alphabet three times and back again by the time the locksmith finally arrived, a good hour and a half later. I was singing at the top of my lungs by then, and didn't hear his key tapping against the ice-encrusted window. All I saw was a pair of red-rimmed eyes under big white bushy brows through my windshield, and I was drunk enough to think of Santa Claus. "Door," I said, pointing. "'s locked."

While he fiddled with one key after another, I asked him all about his work, about life in Santa Fe, about life in general. The old manic craving to know everything was fierce upon me; but luckily, I'd found a willing participant. In fact, I could barely ask my questions before he answered them, at length and in depth. It hit me that he was talking even faster than I was, and that his answers didn't sound quite right. There was something wrong with him, something slightly but significantly off. I looked at him while he was talking and realized that he was younger than I thought. And practically toothless. A single front tooth was framed by two stragglers at the bottom. The rest of the gum was raw and black, like a thick slice of calves' liver. And his eyes weren't just red, they were bloody, the whites shot through with virulent streaks.

Even through the heavy haze of tequila, I heard a warning

bell go off. Step back, I said to myself. Get formal. Slow it down. But we were already well into this strange rhythm: me asking, him answering, me listening hard with all of my body. I didn't know how to stop it, and was worried about offending him. Before I could figure out what to do, his supply of keys ran out. He was stumped. The only thing left to do was break the window.

I loved the idea of smashing glass at that moment. I wanted to do it, but he refused. Wrapping his hand in a greasy old rag, he told me to stand back and close my eyes. Then he bashed the pane once, twice, and on the third blow the glass tinkled onto the tile floor. There's nothing quite like breaking something—the law, a pane of glass, whatever—to embolden a manic mood. "This calls for a drink," I said, as he unlocked and opened the door.

I laid it all out: shot glasses, lime wedges, a shaker of salt and a newly opened fifth of tequila. Since this was probably the last toast I would ever make, I wanted to say something profound, but more than that, I wanted the drink. "Here's to breaking through," I said. When we clinked our glasses, I saw a patch of blood on his shirtsleeve. "You must have cut yourself on the window," I told him. "Sit down, and I'll take care of it."

"It's nothing," he said, pulling his arm away.

"Sit down," I repeated. Two years of taking care of an increasingly infantile father had given me a competent, no-nonsense air of authority when it came to nursing. He sat down, started unbuttoning his cuff, then stopped.

"I can't," he said. "A lady like you shouldn't see this."

"I've seen blood before," I said, laughing.

"It's not that."

"I'm sorry," I said. "Are you burned?"

"No," he said, squirming.

"Scarred?"

"Not really."

I reached over and put my hand on his sleeve. "Then don't be silly. You're bleeding all over my table."

Without looking at me, he finished unbuttoning his cuff and rolled up his sleeve, thereby exposing, from wrist to bicep, the single greatest display of pornographic tattooing I had ever seen on one man's body.

"I'm like this all over," he said. "I used to do drugs. My judgment wasn't so hot back then."

Inadvertently, his bicep flexed, sending the fat couple engraved across it into a copulating spasm. I felt my face flush red, but I couldn't look away. It was grotesque but mesmerizing in a freakish, carnival side-show way. And strangely innocent: as devoid of sexual appeal as the Sunday funnies.

I couldn't help myself. I burst out laughing, and told him I'd seen far worse on my travels. He didn't respond, nor would he meet my eye. I started to clean the small cut on his upper forearm, hoping to relax him, but if anything, the contact made him more nervous. "I'm so sorry," he kept saying. "If I could, I'd burn them all off."

"It's okay, really. Hold still."

"No, I'm hideous," he insisted. "Sometimes I just want to die."

There are lots of easy ways to respond to a statement like that—superficial, cheery bits of wisdom—but the irony slowed me down. Here I was, just waiting for this poor man to leave so I could finish killing myself by midnight; and I was supposed to reassure him of the sanctity of life? I poured us both another shot of tequila.

He pushed his glass away and shook his head. I saw a tear begin to form at the corner of his eye. Toothless, tattooed freak or not, he was suffering, and I knew only too well how that felt. I turned his arm over, exposing his wrist with its dancing, fully erect horned devil. I moistened the area with tequila, sprinkled it with a little salt, then bent down and licked between the tendons. Then I tossed back the shot, slammed the glass down on the table and sucked on my lime.

"That's what I think of your silly tattoos," I said. "Now have a drink. It's Christmas Eve."

Manic intentions are always good; manic consequences, almost never. I hadn't really meant anything sexual by my gesture. I just meant it kindly, one injured animal licking another's wounds. But then he stood up all at once and grabbed me by the arms, pulling me close to him and kissing me full on the mouth. I tried to break loose, but his grip was too strong, his mouth too insistent. I didn't want sex. I just wanted to talk for a minute or two, then I wanted to die. Plus his mouth tasted foul—dark and sour—and I couldn't get rid of the image of those liverish gums. A strong wave of revulsion swept through me, part tequila, part bile. I struggled once again to get free. I felt his hold loosen, took a dizzy

step backward, and heard "No!"—the single word "No!"—and
I don't know which one of us said it before the world went
black.

I woke several hours later, sprawled across my bed,
strangely stiff and sore and damp all over. I was alone. When
I reached down to pull up the comforter, my fingers grazed
my thighs and I felt a familiar cold, wet stickiness. I must have
started my period, I thought, but then I smelled sweat—not
a sweat I knew, but a man's sweat. My inner thighs were
throbbing, almost too sore to move, but I looked down at them.
They were smeared with blood, fresh red bruises just beginning
to shine through.

It really shouldn't have mattered so much. I would be
leaving this body for good, I kept telling myself, as soon as I
could get up and swallow the waiting pills. But it did matter. It
mattered a lot. In the same way that I wanted to leave a neat,
spotless house, so I wanted a clean death. No loose, messy ends
left trailing behind me, and especially no good-byes, not
even to my innocence. I'd already said more than my share of
good-byes.

I didn't want to remember, and I certainly didn't want
to feel, but unbidden, unwanted, the tears started to flow.
With them the memories came flooding back: the jagged
edge of a broken blue bottle, waving back and forth before
my eyes before it disappeared between my legs; a heavy arm
straddling my windpipe; a quick shallow breath in my ear. And

everywhere the little devils dancing, rippling across the surface of his skin, my skin, ours.

I looked down again at the mosaic of blood on the sheets. So much blood, it couldn't all have come from the lacerations on my thighs, which looked fairly shallow. No, there must have been a deeper wound. I reached down and gingerly probed between my legs. My fingers came up slick with fresh blood. There's always a deeper wound somewhere, if you look for it.

I lay back onto the pillow, exhausted. But the physical pain didn't bother me anymore. It was dwarfed by a monstrous wave approaching, the tsunami that I'd been trying to avoid ever since I'd arrived in Santa Fe. I shut my eyes tight; I bit my lip; but I was overwhelmed by the realization that for the first time in my life, I was utterly and completely alone.

"If only Daddy were alive," a voice inside me pleaded. He would have saved me from all of this: not just the evil man with his jagged blue bottle, but the dangerous manias that led me to all these men, and the suicidal depressions that followed. If only Daddy were alive, none of this would have happened. There would be no Santa Fe.

If only Daddy were alive. . . . The truth is, he wouldn't have saved me from any of it. Not the manias, not the depressions, and none of the consequences, because he simply refused to believe that the disease even existed. "It's all in your head," he would say to me, without the slightest tinge of irony. He didn't believe in psychiatry. He believed in bootstraps—as in, pull yourself up by your own bootstraps and get on with your life.

And in the end, he didn't even believe in that. He didn't even believe in me.

The moment I had tried the hardest to forget suddenly snapped back to life in full sensory detail, down to the sharp, astringent smell of the hospital room. It had been a long night for both of us. The cancer had spread to the bones by then, and even the morphine drip couldn't keep the pain at bay for very long. For the past ten days I'd been sleeping on a cot by my father's bedside and living out of a suitcase, hastily packed while I'd waited for the paramedics to arrive. I barely knew if it was day or night anymore, except by the number of pills that I took.

I was dutifully counting out that morning's supply, a good double handful, when I looked up and noticed my father's eyes upon me. I bent over the bed to kiss him good morning, but he turned his head abruptly away. "What's wrong, Daddy?" I asked. "Do you want the nurse?"

He nodded, and I pressed the call button. His eyes fluttered and closed, but his breathing sounded regular, so I sat back down and continued counting out my pills. When the charge nurse arrived a few minutes later, I gently shook my father awake. "She's here, Daddy. The nurse. What did you want?" His eyes were cloudy and his face looked odd, the skin bloodless and gray; but when he sat up and spoke to the nurse, his voice was surprisingly strong. He gestured toward the bedside table. "There's a document in the top drawer there," he said. "And I need a pen."

The nurse opened the drawer and took out the paper. I knew what it was, because I'd helped my father's lawyer get it witnessed and notarized. The nurse pulled a pen from her pocket and handed it to my father, along with the will. Then she turned to leave.

"No, you stay," he said. "Someone should see this." With shaking, palsied fingers he uncapped the pen and began to cross my name off every page on which it appeared.

"She's a drug addict," he said to the nurse. "Just look at all those pills." The nurse looked at me. I still had my morning's supply in my hand, and I instinctively tried to close my fingers around them. But there were far too many, and they all spilled out onto the floor. "It's for manic depression," I started to explain, but my father stopped me.

"I put her through Vassar, I put her through law school, and all she is now is a goddamned drug addict. Who'd have believed it—my little girl." Then he lowered his head back onto the pillow and started to moan softly.

The nurse, bless her, busied herself with the bedside tray. "It's time for your medication now," she said to my father, as she fed him dose after dose of brightly colored pills, a rainbow of pharmacology, pretty but no longer of much use. Exhausted from swallowing, he closed his eyes and slept.

I was there when he woke, a few hours later; and I was there when he died, the following week. At his funeral, I prayed for the strength to forgive him his faults, and I thought that I had succeeded. But flat on my back in Santa Fe, too bruised and too beaten to fight my own feelings, I knew better. I could forgive my father for disinheriting me. I could forgive him for refusing to believe that I was ill. I could even forgive him for not protecting me from the world—how could he, when he couldn't even protect me from himself? But I couldn't, no matter how hard I tried, forgive him for leaving me alone.

A deep, resonant "bong" chimed through my thoughts, as the clock in the next room struck the half hour. Only thirty more minutes to midnight; only thirty more minutes to die. Remembering had made me more eager than ever. Death wasn't the easy way—it was the only way out, it seemed to me, or else I would remember forever. Riding a sudden surge of energy, I jumped out of bed, stumbling as the pain caught up to my senses. On the way to the bathroom, I fell once, hard, and almost stayed there on the thick Berber carpet. But then I forced myself to stand up straight and start swallowing: handful after handful of pills, tossed back with increasingly sloppy swigs of tequila.

Twenty-five minutes later, and three-quarters of the way through my stockpile, I no longer felt the pain, inside or out. My head started nodding in tacit submission, but I slapped my cheeks and chewed my tongue and dug my nails into my palms until the pain startled me awake again. Then I commanded my arm to keep on grabbing, and my throat to keep on swallowing . . . until finally, finally, I held the very last pink-and-green capsule between my fingers, and downed it with the very last drop I hoped I would ever taste of tequila.

My legs slowly slithered out from under me, and I pressed my face gratefully against the cold tile floor, staring up at Christmas through the clerestory window. The last thing I remembered was the clock striking twelve; and a single stubborn snowflake clinging to the windowpane, refusing to let go.

I didn't know whether I would end up in Heaven or Hell, or at least in Purgatory. Instead I woke up in County General, strapped to a gurney, covered in a foul mixture of charcoal and vomit, and retching uncontrollably. I knew it wasn't Heaven, because they kept asking for my insurance. I suspected it wasn't Hell, either, because the attending physician had kind blue eyes and kept patting my hand. "You're alive," he said. "We found you just in time. You're a very lucky girl." And so I knew that it was Hell after all. I hadn't made it. It would be years before I could ever muster together the pills, the opportunity, the money to make another attempt on this grand a scale. This was no gesture. It was genuine despair, and it had failed me.

When I finally got the tubes out of my throat two days later, the nurse gave me a little pad to write on. "Why?" was all I could think of to say. "Why, why, why?" The sweet attending physician finally caught on. "Why are you still alive?" he asked me. I nodded emphatically.

He flipped through my chart. "All I know is that the paramedics were called on Christmas morning. It seems that a young man, a locksmith I think, came by to replace a broken pane of glass at your house, and he found you unconscious. He saved your life."

"Now, about these other injuries. The police have been waiting to talk to you about them. You've got some pretty nasty cuts and bruises down there. Do you know what I'm referring to?"

I nodded.

"Do you want to talk about it?"

I looked back up at those sympathetic sky blue eyes and

shook my head slowly, sadly, and with absolute finality. If my assailant was also my savior, so be it. Perhaps my doubting father could also be my dearest love. I wondered why I, of all people, had never realized it before. The world is essentially bipolar: driven to extremes but defined by flux. Saints are always just a stumble away from sinners. Nothing is absolute, not even death.

Despite the pink Xanax cloud that was fogging my mind, I knew I had hit on something important. All my life I'd been fighting my own private battle of extremes, with little success—so little that I was about to usher in the New Year from a hospital bed, in thick leather restraints. Manic depression was more than a mental disease: it was a mind-set, it colored everything. The world should be one way or another, I thought. Men either made you safe, or they made you bleed. If they weren't gods, they were villains, and it didn't matter if they came at you with bottles, or they came at you with disbelief: either way, you bled.

It was rigid, unnatural thinking. Life was fuzzier than that. I thought of my father, and the perfect smoke rings he used to blow at my command, the endless hours he spent rubbing my back when I had asthma in the middle of the night, and the thousand and one stories that he told me from his big brown chair—cigarette in one hand, whiskey in the other, and me on his lap, in my heaven. It was impossible not to know that he loved me; and that his love had conditions; and that it was still love. The trick was remembering that enormous word *and*.

The nurse came in to adjust the IV, and handed me a box of tissues on her way out. I was crying, my face and chest soaked with tears: tears of resignation, of reluctant compromise. Nothing was absolute, not even despair. I didn't want this life that I'd been given back, but it was a gift nonetheless, and Christmas gifts should always be opened and honored. I would put death aside a little longer, for now, or at least until I understood why I was still alive.

2

I was a star in the making—cold and chilly, with
a calculated twinkle. It was a favorite conceit of mine always to
have fresh flowers in my office, a touch of femininity to offset
my no-nonsense pinstripes and neutered smile. And not just a
single token rose, either, but armfuls of the rarest, most fragrant
or flamboyant blooms I could find: red parrot tulips, delicately
scalloped at the edges; or orchids so fleshy they bordered on
the obscene.

I justified the expense by telling myself that it was good
client relations. Any attorney who could afford hothouse tulips
in December must look like she is doing something right. In
truth, it was simply camouflage, something to hide behind,

to divert attention. At that point in my career, I could easily afford to blow a few hundred bucks a month on flowers. What I couldn't afford was scrutiny.

The rumor around the office, which I didn't discourage, was that I had a wealthy boyfriend. Little did my office know that depression was my secret admirer, and had been for years, long before I ever started practicing law. I never knew when depression would come to call, or for how long, or how dangerous it would be. I only knew that I had to keep it secret, or else. Or else what, I wasn't quite sure, nor was I willing to find out. So the flowers had to stay fresh and pure. I couldn't allow a hint of darkness or decay around me, at least nothing that couldn't be masked by a Casablanca lily. I gave my secretary a standing order to change the water in all the vases daily, and to discard anything that looked to be dead or dying.

There would always be more, I figured. So long as none of the partners ever found out that I didn't have a clue what I was doing as a lawyer, most of the time; that I hated every moment of this existence and every one of their faces; and that the most fragile thing in that office was not, by far, the tulips . . . so long as they just came in, dumped off a file, said "Nice flowers," and left without noticing the deep purple circles under my eyes or the mound of wet wadded Kleenex under my desk, so long as we all agreed not to look too close, or to ask too many questions, there would always be more flowers.

Call it superstition. Call it strategy. Whatever I was doing, it apparently worked, because one April afternoon a few years before my father died I was asked to join the team of lawyers working on the firm's big Michael Jackson case. Our first order of business was to find an expert witness to testify that Michael's songs were not "substantially similar" to any of the plaintiff's songs. We needed a musicologist of the first degree, someone who would impress a jury not just with his expert credentials but with his demeanor, his sincerity, and his innate likeability.

Twenty lunches later, we'd narrowed the field down to two stellar candidates. One was a famous university professor, well known and well respected in the insular world of entertainment expert witnesses. The other candidate (let's call him Joe) also had impressive degrees, but he was twenty years younger and still had hair—lots of it, tied back in a long, neat ponytail. Plus he was a practicing musician, on the road ten months of the year with a band that had known better days, but was still hot enough to command its roadies' respect. As the junior attorney on the litigation team, I felt it was my role to inject some youth into the lawsuit. This was, after all, rock and roll we were defending. So naturally I was leaning heavily toward Joe. It didn't hurt that his band's biggest single had also been the theme of my high school prom. Impressed as I was with his credentials, I was still just a few years shy of a crush.

The day Joe was to be introduced to the rest of the team dawned bright, hot, and sunny, which cinched my choice of restaurants for the big meeting. Where else but The Ivy: that homey little ersatz cottage on North Robertson, that vine-covered nest of vipers where the industry elite meet and mingle over fresh blood and crab cakes. I'd told the team in a preparatory memo that in my opinion, Joe struck just the right note with his unique blend of musical

expertise and showmanship. And sure enough, he showed up
looking professorial but hip in a crisp, black Armani jacket
and well-worn jeans. I could have kissed him. I could have
kissed everyone, it was going so well. By the time our crab
cake entrees arrived, our table was convulsed in laughter,
one anecdote leading to the next in a seamless flow of one-
upmanship. I caught glimpses of the people at other tables
watching us, wondering who we were.

We lingered so long over crèmes brûlée and cappuccinos
that the angle of the sun started shifting to the west, and the
patio began to grow cool. Slipping on his suit jacket, one of
the senior partners asked about the time. "Almost four," I said.
"Are you serious?" Joe said, surprised. I assured him that I was.
"Shit," he said. "I forgot to take my lithium."

The next few minutes are engraved in slow motion on my
synapses. Joe excused himself to get his medication from his
car. Nobody said a word until he got past the gate. And then
the table exploded. Senior partners don't laugh easily, and
record execs are even harder to amuse. But for the next few
minutes, until they spied Joe coming back through the gate,
you'd have thought *lithium* was the funniest word on this
earth.

I wasn't in any position to evaluate the wit. All I could hear,
doglike, was the tone: contempt. And all I could think was, what
would they say if they saw the pharmaceutical cornucopia that I
am carrying around right now in my purse? If plain old lithium
was good for such a belly laugh, they'd die of hilarity over my
dozen assorted mood stabilizers, antidepressants, antianxiety
agents, and atypical antipsychotics.

I had often wondered what would happen if the firm ever found out about my mental illness. Now I knew. I knew without having to be told that Joe was strictly history from that point on, that he didn't have a chance in hell to act as Michael Jackson's expert witness or to have any affiliation whatsoever with our firm in the future. And I knew, with certainty, that I would have to tell him.

While everyone else laughed, I flashed through my options: (1) I could defend poor Joe, reminding my colleagues of his credentials, his reputation, and his prelithium impression; (2) I could defend manic depression, educating these influential men about the importance of battling stigma whenever possible; or (3) I could simply say nothing and wake up tomorrow knowing that I was one step closer to making partner, and one step farther away from myself.

I faced my future unadorned and realized that I wasn't quite ready to give up the fairy tale yet. Not the one about making partner—looking at these men sitting next to me, I knew that I would never be one of them. Believe it or not, I wanted to be callous, too, to be hard enough never to care, but I wasn't. The truth was I was soft deep down, where the really hard decisions are made. I knew that I would cry over what happened to Joe.

No, the only real fairy tale I couldn't relinquish was the one where I wake up one fine sunny morning to discover that the spell is broken, the curse is lifted, and I am not bipolar anymore. Manic depression was not my identity back then. It was simply something I had, like a nasty flu or poor credit. I wasn't even convinced it was real, most of the time. I just knew that whatever it was, it was all my fault, and I didn't like to look too closely at that.

My choice was made. To defend Joe would be an act of solidarity with the disease—symbolic, subtle, but internally unmistakable. And I wasn't about to sacrifice my future for something I didn't really believe in, that might magically go away any morning now. So when the others laughed, I threw back my head and chortled. I listened to their jokes with apparent avidity for the next few minutes. And when Joe returned to the table I, like everyone else, avoided his eyes.

It took me a whole week to get up the courage to meet with Joe in my office and tell him the bad news. I didn't mention the lithium. I made up a story about old-fashioned execs wanting old-fashioned experts. All the time I was lying, though, I wanted to warn Joe to be more careful, to remind him that high-profile jobs demand low-profile lives. But mostly, I think I wanted to confess: to obtain his forgiveness and absolution for the sin of hypocrisy that was still eating away at my hopelessly Catholic soul.

Instead, I offered him flowers: a glorious bunch of daffodils, fresh from the flower market that morning. Forced blooms, the florist had called them, trying to justify the price tag. Forced blooms: flowers made to bloom early, before their time. It sounded painful, but they were worth every penny. I would have paid anything at that point for a graceful good-bye.

Joe left with his daffodils. I grew sick of the sight of myself, day after day, pretending to join in the lithium jokes that continued to circulate around the office until they were finally succeeded by Prozac jokes. I began avoiding other members of the litigation team, coming in later and later until eventually I was doing almost all of my work at night. I started giving away my arrangements to the graveyard cleaning crew, first a stem or two, then a handful, then whole bunches at a time; until one afternoon I arrived at the office and discovered I was completely out of flowers and had forgotten to order more.

I picked up the telephone and dialed the florist, then put it down at the first ring. There weren't enough flowers in the world, I realized, to beautify this office, this life, or this lie that I was perpetuating. I picked up the phone again and dialed another number: the headhunter who had been chasing me for the past six months. "Listen," I said. "There's something you should know about me before we talk, because it's going to make a difference where I go and what I do. I have—" I checked myself. "No, I *am* manic-depressive. So what do you think about that?"

"So's my cousin," he said, not missing a beat. "And do you know . . ." he rattled off the names of three top lawyers at rival entertainment firms, with whom I had worked closely in the past. "But I'm not actually sure you should tell anyone you've got it," he said.

"Of course I shouldn't," I said. "That's why I'm going to." Then I smiled, a real smile. Stories don't always have to end happily, I realized. Sometimes it's just enough that they end, to make way for new stories. I looked down at the legal pad next to my phone and realized that I had sketched a perfect daffodil.

3

I was sitting in the head and neck surgeon's
sleek art moderne waiting room, looking out his wraparound
windows at an endless expanse of sun-flecked ocean, and
feeling unaccountably happy. I'd never been there before,
never met Dr. Cameron, had no idea what he was going to
say about the mysterious swelling in my face and neck that
had thoroughly baffled my internist and endocrinologist and
resisted every antibiotic in their arsenal. The word *tumor* was
mentioned, and in fact that's why I was there, to talk about
tumors and MRIs and CAT scans. Big, scary words, but I was
focused on the small things. I noticed that when the sun hit
the watercooler just right, it made rainbow wallpaper.

There shouldn't have been any sun. It was half past four
on the last day of November, but the sky was relentlessly,
brilliantly blue. I could feel the sunlight through my clothes,
dilating my pores and flushing my pasty, winter-white skin. I
could feel the little hairs along my arms and the back of my
neck start to ripple with pleasure like wind-stroked wheat
and—

Oh my God . . . the little hairs.

Most of the time I barely noticed that I had any body hair
at all. Like most redheads, mine was very fine and delicate,
almost invisible to the eye and soft to the touch. I never had
to worry about waxing or bleaching. I remembered to shave
my legs only if I was feeling particularly sexy in the shower,
which wasn't very often or likely back then. Since my father's
death and my suicide attempt in Santa Fe, the depressions had
become longer and deeper and harder to forget. But innocuous
as the little hairs might have seemed, they were my manic
trip wires. Inevitably, when the chemical balance in my brain
started to shift, they were the first to alert me to it. As soon
as I felt them come alive again, I knew that the depression
was finally lifting. I knew that it was hypomania, heavenly
hypomania at last.

The little hairs loved hypomania: the world was suddenly
all about textures and tastes and sensations, too many and too
much to be ignored. It was all so wickedly delicious, actually
the best part of being bipolar, until my nipples protested
against a surfeit of silk and I felt like a blind man faced with
too much Braille. That's when the little hairs turned inward,
prickling and burning at every sensation, until every nerve

in my body was acutely inflamed and I winced at even the slightest whisper of wind against my skin.

But the little hairs were certainly happy that afternoon, content just to sit there soaking up the sun in the surgeon's fancy waiting room. I wondered if I should remind myself of the gravity of the occasion, that this was neither the time nor the place to be feeling so good. Happiness is fine, in its season, but happiness out of season is a sure harbinger of doom. That's why you should never trust a bright blue sky in November. It might tempt you out the door. It might lure you to forget, for a moment or two, that it is in fact the dead of winter—or will be tomorrow, or the next day, but definitely soon.

How could I ever hope to tell a normal person about the terrors of being happy? Unless there was a damned good reason for it, something objective and verifiable like a winning bingo card or a negative biopsy, happiness wasn't a safe harbor for me. It was just another checkpoint on the road to mania. Stop, wait a minute, hold on there—was I happy? And if I was happy, for God's sake, why? Was I doing something inappropriate, a manic precursor like singing show tunes under my breath in public, or breaking the ice in elevators, or winking at random just for the eyelash kisses? Was I enjoying life inordinately?

I had to ask, because what felt like happy now might well be *too* happy in a minute—and we all knew where too happy could lead. You get too happy, you go pick wildflowers in the middle of the night from your neighbor's lawn, wearing nothing but a sneaky grin. You get even happier and you blithely make a left turn on a red light in Van Nuys in front of a couple of cops, with lots of prescription meds rolling around loose in your purse. In my case, it could definitely be illegal to be too happy.

So when the little hairs tickled, or the midwinter sun shone more brightly than usual, or I heard myself actually laughing out loud . . . I stopped, if I still could. I stopped just to see if I *could* stop. Then I ruthlessly pinpointed the moment on the mood scale, skewered it like a dead butterfly. Happiness management was a cruel science. It may have kept me safe from unexpected butterflies, but it killed all the flutter and delight.

And yet I was happy. Sitting there trying to remember the difference between a CAT scan and an MRI, I was happy. Stop, wait a minute, hold on there—why? I could think of a thousand reasons not to smile, but none of them really counted when the sky was pure delphinium blue at half past four in the afternoon on the last day of November. It was absurd, trying to talk myself out of a smile when smiles were so rare with me.

I summoned up the nasty IRS letter sitting on my kitchen table, the latest in a series of doomsday bulletins threatening garnishment, levy, and seizure of all my assets. I knew I didn't owe the money they wanted, but I was having a hard time establishing why. My finances, so intermingled with my father's, had fallen apart after his death. I had proof of nothing, except for my illness, and the IRS wasn't interested in that. Short of dousing my letterhead in blood, I had nothing left to say.

I squeezed my eyes shut against the problem, squeezed them tight and hard until a familiar acid moisture started to gather in the corners. I could still cry. That was reassuring, I thought, as a lone tear strolled down my cheek. Was I happy?

No, but I was rather enjoying being unhappy for the moment. Leave me alone.

But I wasn't alone. I was never alone. My nagging fishwife of a conscience was hissing in my ear, the same old mantra: "Stop. Wait a minute. Hold on there. . . ." If I really was happy, God help me, and why? For once, I thought I knew the answer: generic aripiprazole, brand name Abilify.

Aripiprazole. Ari-PIP-ra-zole. It was a silly name, froth on my tongue. Just saying it made me giddy. I'd been taking the drug for two weeks, and I still couldn't pronounce it with a straight face. AriPIPrazole! "Abilify" wasn't much better. Was drug-induced happy still happy? Was it the right kind of happy? Did it count? As long as it didn't land me in jail or in a strange man's bed, I really didn't care. I'd take happy any way it came—prescription strength, if necessary.

The receptionist opened the door, called out my name, then led me down the hall into an exam room. The doctor's surgical instruments were laid out in neat, gleaming rows on white linen, a perverted place setting. But this was no picnic. This was serious business, and the man who could pronounce my doom was about to walk through the door.

But the door opened and doom entered, and I was once again unaccountably happy. Nobody ever told me that Dr. Cameron was a dead ringer for Montgomery Clift. You'd think they would have mentioned a little thing like that when you scheduled your first appointment. It certainly would have made the long wait more tolerable. I'm waiting for Montgomery Clift, you could have told yourself as the quarter hour stretched to a half, the half to a whole, and so forth, until it was nearing the end of the last day of November and you were the only patient left in the waiting room.

Dr. Cameron apologized at once for the long delay. An unexpected hospital admission, emergency surgery, something like that. I wasn't listening. His handshake was as warm as his smile and almost as kind as his eyes. This was not at all the cursory "me doctor, you patient, where chart" type of greeting I'd come to expect from first appointments. He held my gaze, and my hand, a half-dozen heartbeats longer than I was prepared for. Not necessarily an inappropriate amount of time, but long enough for the little hairs on the back of my neck to crackle and for a deep, rosy flush to spread from my neck to my chin to my cheeks. Thank God I'd been running a fever, and I could blame the heat on that.

Or could I? Dr. Cameron didn't take my temperature. He didn't even look at my chart. He looked in my eyes, then reached out and smoothed my hair back behind my ear. He picked up one of the utensils (a medium-sized one, somewhere between a shrimp fork and a speculum) and blew on it. "To warm you up," he said with a wink as he gently inserted it into my ear, and I tried simultaneously to tame my pulse and to place his familiar aftershave.

"Beautiful," Dr. Cameron said at last, returning my hair to its original place. I didn't know whether he meant my inner ear or my hair or me or the moment, and I really didn't care. I tried to concentrate on something totally asexual and sterile like the acoustical ceiling tiles or the autoclave, but then he was tickling the cilia in my nose and it was all I could do not to snort with rapture.

The little hairs were far too happy. I knew that I should stop and worry about that, but I also knew that the throat exam was coming next, with all its symbolic portent, and I needed to stay in the moment. So while Dr. Cameron explored my mouth and tongue with his long silver probe, his lips just a fraction of an inch away from mine, I rid my brain of all extraneous thoughts and multiplied ceiling tiles fast and furiously in my head until he was done.

"Good news," he said, stepping back and beaming down at me. "I don't think it's a tumor. The inflammation's too symmetrical—here, and here." He stroked both sides of my face, from earlobe to midthroat, as he talked. "No doubt it's all the medications you're taking. They've kept you so dehydrated that your body is trying to hold on to all the fluids it possibly can. Which would explain this swelling in your parotid and submandibular salivary glands—here, and here, and under here." More strokes. Who knew Montgomery Clift had such a delicate touch? But then, wasn't Montgomery Clift gay?

I looked closely at Dr. Cameron, who had finally stopped stroking my face and throat and was jotting down notes in my chart. He was awfully good-looking—not just movie star handsome, *gay* movie star handsome. Could it be that the heat between us was only in my imagination? I'd like to think that at forty-two my body was wise enough to know, viscerally, when sex was in the air. A few extra seconds of handshake, eye contact that lingered just a bit beyond necessary, a touch gentle enough to be a caress in other circumstances: these were all excellent clues. But the real mystery wasn't whether Dr. Cameron was actually gay. It's whether I was actually

manic. Maybe the electricity in the room was just manic
fallout, the residue of my supercharged sensibilities. Maybe
the heat was just a fever, and strictly *my* fever, at that.

But then he looked up from the chart and flashed a
great big movie star grin at me, all gleaming white teeth and
charisma, and I knew that I didn't give a damn whether he was
gay or straight. He was gorgeous. I'd just have to work all the
harder to win him over, that was all. I used to be pretty good at
persuasion. Over the years I'd developed quite a repertoire of
tricks, little subtleties of voice and eye and carriage that I could
usually count on to sway a hesitant jury, or soothe a recalcitrant
judge. This wasn't much different. I leaned forward in the
chair and looked into the far back reaches of Dr. Cameron's
eyes. Then I smiled, ever so slowly and gradually, without
saying a word—an old ploy that usually made the other person
smile back in anticipation. Everyone loves to hear a secret, the
more secret the better. So I dropped my voice down low and
conspiratorial, and said, "You know, of course, that you look
exactly like my all-time favorite movie star?"

He laughed. "Montgomery Clift? Yeah, I've heard that one
before."

"And not just any Montgomery Clift," I continued.
"Montgomery Clift in *A Place in the Sun*—you know, the one
where he kisses Elizabeth Taylor in that incredible close-up
that goes on and on for what seems like forever, until you can't
believe it ever got past the censors." I tried to restrain myself,
but my eyes wandered down to his lips and waited there for his
reply.

"Not only do I know it," he said. "I actually have a copy

of his original screen test with Elizabeth Taylor. It's a real collector's item. My ex gave it to me for my last birthday."

My ex. He didn't have to say that. My mind quickly calculated the possibilities in that prehyphenate. Not married; possibly not involved. Or, not married but still very good friends with his ex, which was not as good as not involved but was certainly better than married. My eyes moved to his ring finger: bare, no tan line, no telltale indentations on the flesh. A very uninvolved finger.

"Wow, that must be fantastic," I said. "Does he look like you in the screen test? Does he kiss Elizabeth Taylor? Does he kiss anybody? Does he talk about kissing? Wow. I'd sure love to see it sometime."

He put down my chart. "I can tell you're a real fan. I'd be happy to lend it to you—if you promise you'll bring it back next week."

"But . . . aren't we through? I thought you figured out what was wrong with me. Do I have to come back?"

"You don't *have* to come back," he said, and the emphasis stopped my heart. "But I hope you will. At least come tell me what you thought of the tape. I'm in surgery on Mondays and Wednesdays, but Fridays are usually light, especially Friday afternoons after four P.M. Actually, try to come then if you can. You can usually see the sunset from here around that time. It's been absolutely incredible lately. It goes on and on forever— just like the kiss, I suppose." Another pyrotechnic smile.

I started to tell him that there had been no sunset that day, at least none that I had seen; that the waiting room was in fact still relentlessly, brilliantly sunny and hot at half past four that afternoon. I was seriously smitten, and I wanted to tell him, to warn him, that it was a bright blue sky in November and we should both be very, very careful . . . but he'd already excused himself and left the room to get the tape.

Stop, wait a minute, hold on there. I didn't even have to ask if I was happy, I was terribly, terribly happy and what had just happened? Was terribly happy too happy? And scariest question of all, whatever had I done this time to deserve it? Damn damn damn. If there was one sure sign of mania's approach, it was this secret conviction I got that I was the ultimate arbiter of other people's sexuality, this sudden rush of confidence that no man—or woman, if I so desired—was beyond my jurisdiction.

I pulled out my mirror and started to reapply my lipstick, then I willed myself to stop. No. I resisted the almost physical need to comb my hair, straighten my skirt, check my breath. No, no, no. I didn't have to succumb to the manic whirlwind in my ear, which was urging me to seize any happiness in my grasp because tomorrow I could be worse than dead—I could be depressed. No, I said. I didn't want to grasp at happiness anymore. For once, I wanted happiness just to float gently down and settle on my shoulder.

Dr. Cameron would be back any minute, and I was painfully aware that the part in my hair was crooked, I could feel the asymmetry along my scalp. Looking down, I noticed a little snag in my stocking that I could have easily hid if I had just stood up for a second and tucked it under my skirt. I was pretty sure there was a scuff mark on my left shoe, too, that I would have probably buffed out with a quick spit and polish. But manic seduction with me is all about fixing smudges, pretending that I'm perfect in all the places I'm most flawed. So I forced myself to sit stock-still, and I tried hard not to picture how pale my lips must have looked in the naked light.

Terribly, terribly happy was quickly dissolving into not so terribly comfortable. How absolutely marvelous. How thrilling. Probably nobody but a manic-depressive can understand that putting on the brakes is sometimes far more exhilarating than winning the race. Something was clearly working, and this time I was sure it was the new medication. Abilify was actually nicknamed "Goldilocks" because when it worked, it struck a balance between too much and too little dopamine until it finally, hopefully, hit on the amount that was just right for you.

"Just right." Who would have thought that I would ever be satisfied with "just right," when "more" is always around the next corner? But I knew that manic corner: you had to round it at three times the legal speed limit, and sooner or later a cop would be waiting for you on the other side, eagerly jingling his handcuffs and utterly indifferent to your diagnosis. That was why happiness for me no longer lived in excess. It lived in the absence of: the absence of pain, the absence of depression, the absence of consequences I never intended to incur.

I looked down again at the very visible snag on my thigh—and yes, there was a scuff mark on my shoe—then I straightened up. I felt noble and victorious, resisting the little hairs' call to action. Dr. Cameron returned, patted me on the back and handed me the tape. "Let's have one last look," he said. "Open wide." But my body had gone rigid with propriety and my jaw was practically clenched shut. "Wider," he said. "Come on now, open up wide for me."

It would be hard to resist a line like that even if you were not getting manic, but I did my best. Before Dr. Cameron's aftershave made me forget all my good intentions, the exam was over. He reached down into his pocket and pulled out a lollipop. I swear. A big red lollipop. He handed it to me and laughed at the expression on my face. "This is actually your treatment," he said. "I want you to go out and buy several bags of these when you leave. It's extremely sour and when you suck on it it's going to stimulate the parotid glands' production of saliva. But I warn you, it's going to be very, very uncomfortable. You're going to feel a whole lot worse before you feel better."

For more reasons than you could possibly know, I thought to myself, bending down and sticking the lollipop in my purse. Just forcing myself not to execute a come-hither head toss when I straightened up was almost more than the little hairs could stand. But it was war now, war against all those natural impulses that naturally got me into trouble, and I didn't expect to be comfortable. I stood up and extended my hand, thanking Dr. Cameron for the tape and promising I'd get it back to him as soon as possible. God, his hand felt good in mine. But I pointedly didn't make a definite date, and as of that moment, at least, I figured I'd just return the tape to his receptionist in a few days, and let matters take their own unfettered course from there. I'd put the repertoire of little tricks away, along with all my other nets and snares.

I left the room without a backward glance. The elevator was too slow, so I took the stairs. Ten, eleven, twelve flights down, and the back of my neck still tingled. When I stepped outside, twilight was starting to descend. I automatically headed in the direction of my pharmacy—but then I realized that for the first time in years, I had actually walked out of a doctor's office without any prescriptions to fill. No wildly expensive pills or potions, just permission to buy a big bag of lollipops when I got home.

This must be what life is like for normal people, I thought. No drugs, just candy and bright blue skies in November that presage nothing more than a spectacular sunset. Maybe the Abilify fairy tale was coming true after all, and I really was Goldilocks and this really was a happy ending.

Happily ever after, for once—or at least, happily ever after, for now.

Or, better yet: just right.

4

I have never sinned on purpose. Not that it
mattered now, when the deed was done. I paced the narrow
cell, the cell without bars, without windows, with no
distractions but my own wandering thoughts. I may very
well have turned too late on that left-turn light. I couldn't
remember. I could remember the loudspeaker voice telling me
to pull over and stop the car. But when I looked back in my
rearview mirror, there was no one there. No black-and-white
with the spinning red light on top. No one was there.

   Not until I pulled up to the stop sign, and the pounding on
my windows began. I peered into the dark and saw two faces
with bicycle helmets on. It was ten o'clock at night, it was Van

Nuys, and I was alone and not feeling very well. I took off with the tires squealing. Then at last came the siren, the flashing lights, and the same loud, tinny voice saying "Stop the car immediately. This is the police."

Bicycle cops. I was arrested by bicycle cops.

I had at that point a near perfect driving record: one speeding ticket in seven years—and for a girl with a Porsche, that's pretty damn good. So I wasn't too concerned. Maybe one of my taillights was out. And surely they'd understand why I hadn't pulled over in Van Nuys at ten P.M., all alone and no police car in my rearview mirror.

I forgot about the drugs. Not street drugs, perfectly legal. Prescribed. I kept my doctor's card in my purse, along with the extra pills I always carried for safety's sake. Granted, the pills were also lethal if taken with the wrong foods or medications. MAO inhibitors, they're called, and they're the court of last resort when it comes to manic depression. No doctor ever prescribes MAOIs unless everything else has failed. But I had been through every drug out there, not just in the United States, but Europe, too. I had been through electroshock therapy, and every other kind of therapy known to man. Nothing had worked. When depressed, I was suicidal. When manic, I had the energy to act on those suicidal impulses—and I did. Repeatedly.

So when my doctor prescribed an MAOI, I went along with it. I looked it up in the PDR, and it freaked me out. If I ate anything containing the substance tyramine, I would have a stroke. Tyramine is everywhere: in pizza, red wine, cheese, smoked meats, liver, caviar, and fava beans, just to name a few.

I figured I could live without fava beans, even pizza if I had to. And I had to. I was inches away from the next suicide attempt, and I knew it.

The only problem was, I kept fainting. Mostly when I stood up, but sometimes when I was walking. Never when I was sitting down. So far as we could tell, the drugs made my blood pressure plummet when I stood up, a condition called orthostatic hypotension. I carried a compact blood pressure kit with me, and tried to monitor myself every hour or so. Lately, it hadn't been much help.

I'd fainted everywhere during the past few weeks—at the Third Street Promenade, at the Beverly Hills Public Library, in my boyfriend's arms, in a stranger's arms. Once I passed out on the sidewalk in a not-so-good part of town, and woke to find my purse stolen and my skirt partially unzipped. I passed out walking to Saks in Beverly Hills, and was shaken awake by two cops, who wanted to take me into custody but finally relented once I got my therapist on my cell phone. He explained the situation—that I had never sinned on purpose, and that the medication was prescribed. The cops were nice about it. They even offered to drive me home, but by that time I was fine—coherent, well-mannered, even a little flirty—so they let me go with a warning about walking on public streets while I was taking this medication. A warning. Who ever listens to a policeman's warning? You're just relieved you talked your way out of the mess, even a bit smug about your luck. I should have listened.

When the Van Nuys cops told me to get out of the car, I hesitated, because it meant standing up. "Get out of the car, with your hands in plain view." I pushed myself up by the steering wheel, placed my hands in plain view on the car door, and the world went white again. Then little spots started to swim in front of my eyes, like they always did when I came to. All I could clearly see was the bicycle helmet looming over me: "Stand up and walk in a straight line," it said. "I'm sorry, really, I'd like to. I'm just a little bit dizzy right now. . . ."

A second helmet swam into view, then four arms, and then I was up against the car, and all the hands were patting my body. "It's in my purse," I said. I meant my doctor's number, that would solve everything, just like with those nice cops in Beverly Hills. But this was Van Nuys, and when they dumped my purse out on the sidewalk, all the extra pills spilled out. While I tried to explain, they read me my rights. Just like on TV.

It was everything you've ever seen, and a bit more. The handcuffs bit into my wrists, they were cold, and they made an unexpected snapping sound when they closed shut. The police station was dirty, crowded, and I couldn't place the smell. When they took the mug shot, I didn't know whether to smile or look whipped. But the booking was worst of all. I kept trying to explain, begging them to just let me call my doctor. Or my lawyer, my therapist, my boyfriend. The woman carefully rolling my fingers in the black smudgy ink refused to even look me in the eyes. None of them looked me in the eyes. They focused somewhere around my throat, as if measuring it for a possible choke hold. I started to realize that I wasn't human anymore, that once they'd assigned me a case number, my eyes no longer existed.

Next a woman cop took me into a little room behind the booking desk. She undid the handcuffs, God bless her, and told me to wait there. I thought this was finally cell phone time, they'd certainly taken long enough. But she came back with rubber gloves on, and a little mirror attached to a stick, like a dentist uses to check for cavities.

Still looking anywhere but in my eyes, she held out a metal box. "Shoelaces, belt and watch," she said. I wasn't wearing shoelaces, I was wearing ballet flats. Chanel, my favorites. But they did have little bowties on them, so I took them off. I noticed my hands were trembling. "Now undress." I stared at her. "Do it or else I'll do it for you." I was wearing a summer dress, my Audrey Hepburn dress, I called it. I had no bra on underneath, not even a slip—just summer panties. If I took it off, I would be naked. "What for?" I asked. "Body search." "Wait, you don't understand, it was prescription medication." She took me by the shoulders and turned me around, unzipped my dress, and pulled it over my head. Then she bent me over.

This wasn't happening, it couldn't be; but the rubber fingers were very real. Thank God I couldn't see what was going on back there, or what she saw in the little dental mirror. When it was over, she told me to stand up and wait there. Standing up was scary, because I thought I might faint again, but my head slowly cleared and I stood my ground. She returned a few minutes later with an orange jumpsuit: "Put this on, and wait there." Wait there, wait there. Where the hell else was I supposed to go? "What about my phone call?" I asked, but she had already shut the door behind her.

Orange has never been my color. I had to wear it for a year as a varsity cheerleader, and I looked like hell the whole time. Redheads should almost never wear orange. The jumpsuit was far too big, and scratchy as a Brillo pad, but I just rolled up the legs and sleeves and waited there.

The trembling worried me. It was more than fear, it was a sign of something going chemically wrong. I tremble when I'm manic, I get light-headed and dizzy, and I sweat. All of which I was doing now. And I could feel the words coming on, the irresistible desire to say all the things spinning around in my head. I needed that phone call; I needed it badly.

A male cop finally opened the door. I saw the handcuffs dangling from his belt, but he didn't put them on me. He just told me to follow him. "What about my phone call?" I asked, but he didn't answer. I followed him down a long hall, through a heavy metal door with iron bars on the window that we had to be buzzed through. On one side of the room was what I knew from TV to be a holding cell, containing half a dozen women still dressed in street clothes, looking bored and a bit disheveled. One of them was reading a book, which for some reason gave me hope.

We kept going, past another metal door with another iron-barred window, down yet another hallway. We finally stopped in front of a third door, also metal but even thicker. This one had no windows. The door guarded a small, maybe 8 x 10–foot room, with a metal bench attached to the longer wall. When the policeman told me to go in and wait there, I gladly entered and sat on the bench, relieved. I assumed the cell phone was coming at last, and they wanted to give me complete privacy.

Until the metal door swung shut, and it clanged. I'd seen enough TV shows to know the meaning of a door that clangs shut. I'd always assumed that it was some kind of enhanced sound effect, but in fact it was even louder, clangier, more final than I had imagined.

It was long past time for my medication. I had been on my way home to take it when I was pulled over. The MAOIs required precise dosing to maintain a safe and effective level in the blood. It's a religion with me, taking my pills on time. I don't want to mess with the gods, or my brain chemistry. Just because I'm mentally ill doesn't mean I'm crazy.

I should have known that I was getting manic long before my trembling fingers tried to zip up the orange jumpsuit. What, in the name of God and all the saints, was I doing in Van Nuys? I never go to the Valley. Especially not in summer, when it's hot and smoggy. It was coming back to me, in scattered bits and pieces: I had left my house in Benedict Canyon while it was still light. I wanted wildflowers. I always want wildflowers at the beginning of mania, there's something about the illicit search and pluck that thrills me. Wildflowers, you see, don't always grow wild. Not when you're manic.

The best picking was north of my house, where the canyon slowly winds up toward Mulholland Drive, and the real estate values climb proportionately. When you're manic, it's sometimes impossible to change direction. You just go and keep on going. So I must have worked my way up to Mulholland and continued over and down the hill to Van Nuys. I had a vague recollection of sitting in a dim, noisy coffeehouse, surrounded by young men and the constant

pinging of video games. Ordering lattes for us all, treating,
as I always did when I was manic. And flirting. Flirting hard,
with someone, a boy with an accent. That gorgeous dusky boy
from Mombasa, with the desert sheik eyes. The parking lot, the
kiss—no, wait, the kisses. His hands. My car. Did I even ask his
name? Did I ever, when I was manic? Thank God my car had
bucket seats, and a stick shift in between.

I must have fallen asleep from sheer exhaustion because
I don't remember lying down. When I woke, my throat was
achingly dry and my tongue thick and coated. I heard a
knocking on the door, and a key clicking in the lock. A guard
entered, carrying a plastic tray with a banana, a small container
of orange juice, and a slice of bread with a pat of butter on top.
It must have been breakfast time. I had been arrested before
midnight.

"What about my phone call?" I demanded. "I just give
out the food," said the guard, and he placed the tray on the
floor and left. I threw the whole thing at the door, but it barely
made a sound against the reinforced metal. I refused to eat
their lousy food, although I swallowed the orange juice in one
grateful gulp. One of the worst side effects of my medication is
the constant dry mouth. I never go anywhere without a bottle
of water and a half dozen tubes of lip balm. But they had
confiscated all my ChapStick at the desk, and now the corners
of my mouth were starting to crack and bleed. I took the pat
of butter off the tray and smeared it across my lips. It was
time to get crafty; who knew how long I'd be in there. I took
the remaining butter and spread it in my belly button, and in
between my toes, for later.

I had no idea how long I'd been locked in solitary confinement when a guard finally arrived to escort me to the phone. I was worried, of all things, about the butter dripping from my belly button into my pubic area. If they were going to conduct another cavity search, would it look like some kind of melted drug?

But the guard took me to a phone, and stood watch outside while I dialed my therapist's number, which I knew by heart. There was no ring. I hung up and tried again, thinking perhaps my shaking hands had punched the wrong buttons. No ring, again. A third time, and now no dial tone at all.

I opened the door and told the guard that the phone didn't work. Was there another one, or could I get a cell phone? Talking to my throat, he explained that in solo detention you're only allowed one phone call per hour. I could hear my voice rise: "Wait a minute, I've been here all night, and this is the first time I've ever been allowed to call anyone. You're telling me I have to wait another hour before I can talk to my lawyer? To my *lawyer*?!" My brain struggled to remember what the TV shows said about a prisoner's right to one phone call. Did it count if the call didn't go through? Were they supposed to give you another phone? I couldn't remember, nor did my legal training help, since all I knew was entertainment and copyright law.

The guard returned me to the clanging door. I have no idea how long I paced and cried and pounded that damned door before another guard, a woman this time, finally came to get me. Lunch had already gone by, meaning another pat of butter was safely smeared on the cold tile floor where it wouldn't melt. The guard gestured impatiently, but I stood up too quickly and the earth started slipping away. I grabbed her by the arm to steady myself. Never grab a guard by the arm. She jerked back, I fell, and she clanged the door shut again.

The meal was waiting for me on the floor when I came to. Sometimes protein helped ease the shakes, so I carefully peeled off the cheese from the gray thing that might have been meat, and nibbled. A few minutes later, the same woman guard unlocked the door. "Sobered up yet?" she said. I started crying as we walked down the hall, partly in relief that it looked like I was going to get another phone call, and partly in frustration that I couldn't make myself understood. "I'm not drunk," I said. "I'm not even on drugs, they're prescribed. But I need my medication. It's really serious. You have no idea how serious it is." This woman had a genius for ignoring her fellow creatures. "At least look me in the fucking eyes while you're ignoring me, goddamit!" I shouted. And then I knew that a certain line had been crossed, both with the cops and with my own level of sanity. I would never knowingly say "fuck" to a police officer, any more than I would say "fuck" to a judge. Unless I was manic. I was probably manic. Good. The fucking bastards deserved it.

The guard's lips tightened when I swore at her, and she grabbed hold of my elbow, hard, as if to guide me down the hallway. But it wasn't that kind of a touch. It hurt, and no guidance was necessary. We were already there, at the blessed phone booth. I was crying full out while I dialed. When the phone didn't ring, I just hung up and redialed more carefully. And when it didn't ring again, I went even more slowly, saying each number aloud as I pressed it. But when I tried again and there was no dial tone, something exploded inside me, and I lost all control.

When I burst out of that booth, I wasn't afraid anymore. I was a lawyer, a manic lawyer, and there's no scarier beast on earth. I assailed the room with words: "Egregious violation of the Fourteenth Amendment, not to mention 42 U.S.C. section 1983 *and* intentional infliction of emotional distress. You assholes—don't you know that even the union won't save you from this?"

There were at least ten cops in that room behind a glass partition, and I think I must have insulted them all, as a class and individually, by the time they noticed where the screaming was coming from. I saw a vacant phone on a nearby desk. It took me ten seconds to lunge in that direction. It took the guard five seconds to knock me to the floor.

And then she was all over me, all two hundred pounds of her. She forced my head to the floor. It was sticky with what I later realized was my own blood. She jammed one knee against my back, and started hitting. Not with her fist, with the club that hung by her side, next to the cuffs and the keys. I was shaking so badly by then I don't know how she managed to land a solid blow, but she must have been thoroughly trained, because my ribs were exploding one after another, a most thorough and systematic attack.

What was I feeling at that moment? Was I still howling legal curses? All I remember were the sounds, round, hollow, knocking sounds from inside, that might have been my ribs or might have been my head pounding against the floor. I felt no pain, not until later, when the bruises welled up and a thick, itchy scar began to form. Mostly I was worried about the butter. I wondered what she'd do if she found it. I wondered how much longer this would last, if she'd ever get tired. I was tired. The floor was smooth and cold, and I just wanted to lie down and sleep, sleep forever, or until it was over. Sleep and wake somewhere else, in a field of wildflowers, safe and warm.

She stopped at some point, or I fell asleep, or I fainted. It doesn't matter. The butter was still there when I was tossed back into my cell, and I tried to spread it on my bleeding forehead. It had congealed and was turning rancid.

Some time later, they wheeled a cart with a phone on it into my cell. I connected with my lawyer at last. He told me to wait there—again, wait there—and he would be over within the hour. After posting a bond, I was finally released. It was fourteen hours since I had been pulled over.

My lawyer later told me that the Penal Code mandates that a prisoner be allowed to contact his attorney within three hours of his arrest and that any medication request has to be reviewed by the doctor on call. It didn't matter. The thing inside that used to care—that got indignant, outraged, that insisted on its rights—had been beaten out of me. It just didn't matter anymore.

Nothing has ever been the same for me since that endless moment on the cold stone floor. Nothing ever will be. I know now that I am touchable, that I am not immune. You grow up separated from the people on the bus, or the people on the street, by a glass wall of money, education, a profession. You never think it could be you when you watch that poor black guy being beaten up by the cops. It's just TV. You can barely remember his name now—Arthur King? Robert King? Rodney. You are Rodney King, and it doesn't even show in the mirror.

Maybe it's worse when you're a lawyer, and you know what rights are being violated. Maybe it's not, because when you get out, there's another lawyer waiting to defend you. I ultimately got off with a reduced sentence—a "wet reckless," which cost me a bundle but didn't really inconvenience my life. But I still hesitate to take my shirt off and reveal my scars to a new lover. I hesitate to bare myself at all.

5

I knew I was getting a little bit manic when my
next-door neighbor's drums started driving me mad. Even
though I wasn't practicing law full-time anymore, I still had
to pay the rent. I'd taken on a petition for habeas corpus, and
the deadline was looming. But for the past two hours, I'd
been assaulted by an incessant thump-thump-da-thump, so
loud it made my bedroom windows shiver. I'd been lenient
so far about the late-night jam sessions, the early-morning
piano scales, and the *White Album* playing over and over in
an endless homage to the 1960s. I'd been lenient because I'd
heard that my neighbor was a big-time songwriter and record
producer, and I loved living next door to a big-time songwriter

and record producer. Somehow it made my own rent seem a bit less obscene.

But when you're heading up toward mania, the slightest sensation hotwires your nerves. Sound is noise, sunshine is glare, and it takes all of your self-control not to just slice that mosquito bite clean off your ankle. That morning the prick of the hairbrush against my scalp had been so excruciating I'd thrown the brush in the toilet. I've thrown a lot of things in the toilet on my way up to mania—not all of them visible, or easily replaced.

Forty-two more minutes of thump-thump-da-thump, and the little hairs along the back of my neck and arms were bristling with outrage. Something had to be done—now, this instant, before the blood started pulsing out my ears in rhythmic spurts. Anger spun me into action before I could even ask myself why now or what if. Between beats, between breaths, I made up my mind to confront the bastard face-to-face. In retrospect, it must have been that dizzy, precarious moment when my chemical balance starts to topple, when almost stable turns into almost not. One minute I was contemplating soundproofing the windows with Scotch tape, the next I was pawing through my closet, looking for the sexiest confront-your-neighbor outfit I could find.

You get beautifully and painfully thin on the road up to mania. Eating simply doesn't occur to you because there are too many other thoughts occupying your mind, important thoughts, thoughts that could change the world if only you could stop long enough to jot them down. So I was thin enough that day to wear those sleek black jeans. They were a bit trashier than my usual attire, but they made the perfect foil for my favorite green silk shirt, the one that looked so delicate against my fair white skin, that is, until the light hit just right and the silk became completely transparent.

"Nipples are natural," I said to myself as I buttoned up the cuffs and slipped into my shoes. I'd settled on a pair of plain black flats as a concession to propriety, which means that I couldn't have been all the way manic. True mania never steps out the door in anything less provocative than spike heels or sling-backs.

Tight jeans, visible nipples, and sensible flats: an odd assemblage of personalities, but it wasn't what I was really wearing when I marched up the street to my neighbor's gate. In my mind's eye, I was dressed for battle, in the cruel gray suit that I wore only to federal court, and then only for do-or-die cases; and the black patent leather pumps that I purposefully bought a size too small, just to keep me mean.

Facing the enemy gate, I smoothed my hair, straightened up, and squared my shoulders. It was an odd, echoing sensation. The motion was as automatic as my speeding pulse. It was all too familiar: I was standing in front of the courtroom door.

My body simply won't forget it, no matter how hard my mind tries: the trickly sweat exhilaration of high-stakes litigation. It had been well over four years since I left the fast track, and much as I missed the money, I knew that I could never safely return to the full-time practice of law. I knew it absolutely; and yet like an alcoholic who remembers the high and never the hangover, my body still craved the pure adrenaline drunk of always playing to win. Winning was what I'd been trained for. It was where I belonged. And through no fault of my own, it was what I did best. So I savored, just for a moment, the pinch of those black patent leather pumps that had never really fit me, not even when I won. Then I steadied my hand and pressed hard on my neighbor's doorbell, just a second or two past polite.

He answered the door. His "Hi there, how ya doin'?" was so soft and sweet and mellow it sounded like he was singing. Or stoned? And then I saw the green eyes. Green-eyed men do something to the cartilage in my knees, always have, always will.

"Um, I live next door." I pointed in the wrong direction. "I'm a lawyer."

He nodded, waiting for more. More was not forthcoming. More was jammed in the back of my throat, afraid to come out with something even stupider than "Hi, I'm the lawyer next door."

"Well, thank you, I'm very happy with my representation right now, but I'll certainly keep you in mind," he said. "Why don't you just drop off your card with my housekeeper one of these days, okay? Nice to finally meet you."

I had enough residual anger in me, and more than enough manic irritability, to hear a deliberate insult in even the most innocent remark, no matter how sweetly it was spoken or how green the speaker's eyes. I may not be able to afford this neighborhood anymore, I thought, and no doubt my poor ramshackle little house reflects it. But I'll be damned if anyone's going to insinuate that I'm peddling my

J.D. up and down the street like some overeducated Avon Lady. So I summoned forth The Voice I used to use for such polite venom as "my worthy opponent," or "Your Honor, I respectfully dissent."

"Look," said The Voice. "I've got a major filing deadline coming up, and there's no way I'll make it if I don't get a break from those god-awful drums. I mean, no offense, but it's been going on for hours now. I've tried everything—ear plugs, headphones, you name it, but—"

I was interrupted by another chorus of thump-thump-da-thump. The noise was even louder at the source, I noticed, and out of the corner of my eye I saw with satisfaction that my neighbor's windows were shaking, too.

There was nothing but vibrations between us.

In high-stakes litigation, you have to be fast on your feet, always two beats ahead of your opponent. So I was ready, rattlesnake ready, for whatever the next few seconds might bring. Ready, as always, for battle—but not for laughter. Laughter has no place between proper enemies. And yet he laughed. He leaned back against the gate post and laughed, an honest-to-God, deep from the diaphragm laugh. I think it must have been a stoned laugh, too, because within a few seconds I had caught the high. And for the first time that day, probably several days, the sounds that emerged from inside me had no tinge of anger or irritation.

He reached over and put his hand on my arm. "God, I'm so sorry," he said. "I thought you were . . . I thought you wanted. . . . Anyway, I swear I never even heard those drums until now. I've been in the record business so long I just tune it all out, you know? It's my little boy's birthday today, and I've only got him for the weekend, so I'm probably overindulging as usual. But don't worry, he'll be taking the drums with him tomorrow when he goes back home to his mother. A little unexpected present for her. . . ."

It wasn't really funny, except in a sitcom kind of way, but it set us off again. Silly was such a tremendous relief that I never even stopped to wonder at my sudden and radical shift of mood. At some point, without my even noticing it, defiance had melted away.

"Actually, this is perfect," my neighbor said. "We're having a party right now for Trevor—that's my little boy—and we've got tons of food. Amazing desserts. We'll just have to throw it all away tomorrow, unless you come in and help us out. And you can take some home, as much as you want." He held out his hand. "By the way, my name is Julian."

"I'm Terri," I said, and I slipped my hand into his, trying my best to clasp it like the girl next door and not a lawyer on the make.

Although we were next-door neighbors, the only thing Julian's house and mine had in common was a ZIP code. My bedroom would have fit inside his foyer. His kitchen sink would have swallowed up my bathtub, if I'd had one.

But the real difference between us wasn't size: it was light, light that gleamed and glinted from every direction, caught up and ricocheted around the room by high-tech chrome fixtures and rows of copper-bottomed pots and pans. Light like the light in Julian's house is a luxury few can afford. So I knew that the dozen or so people hanging out in his kitchen were probably high-priced, too. You wouldn't have guessed it from their clothes—in fact, casual bordered on disheveled here and there. But if you knew competitive pretty, and I knew it well, then *res ipsa loquitor*: the evidence spoke for itself. I knew that those practically seamless hair extensions pulled back any-which-way in a plastic barrette must have cost upwards of a thousand dollars. I knew what it meant to have teeny-tiny locked-ring logos imprinted all over your scuffed-up backpack: the teenier the Chanel icon, the loftier the price. But most telling of all was what I didn't see. Not one of the six women in that kitchen, all in their forties and up, had any frown lines between their eyebrows, or laugh lines around their mouths, or little fissures above their lips. *Ergo*: Botox injections at four hundred dollars to start; collagen, at least five hundred a fix; and maintenance essential every three to five months.

Some of the women gave me the up-and-down look. I knew that look; I was giving it back. But with Julian at my side, shepherding the introductions, I felt no need to defend myself. His friends got to meet the girl next door, in the slightly slutty black jeans and the green silk shirt, which had dissolved the moment I stepped into the kitchen light. The men didn't seem to mind my appearance. In fact they were very, very interested in my story about the drums. I don't know what the women thought. After a brief hello, they all went off to a separate little dining nook on the other side of the room.

Julian hadn't been kidding earlier when he said there was way too much food. I counted at least ten different desserts for less than a dozen people, plus a doggie bag or two. I had to admit that they were, as Julian had said, amazing: lemon tarts

topped with edible flowers; a bottomless bowl of English trifle
with real crème fraîche on the side; raisin pudding so steeped
in rum it made my eyes water just to smell it.

Julian sat me down on a bar stool at the center island right
in the middle of all the guys, under a double row of copper-
bottomed cookware (a nice backdrop for a strawberry blonde).
He stacked a plate with helpings of each dessert, and told me
to try one of everything. I wasn't the least bit hungry, although
I knew I should be, who wouldn't be when faced with passion
fruit sorbet and white chocolate–covered strawberries as big as
a fist? I realized that I hadn't eaten a thing that day, or, come to
think of it, the day before. In fact, I couldn't remember the last
time I ate. I knew what that probably meant, sort of, kind of. I
knew that it probably meant I had reached a certain milestone
on the road up to mania: at least three-quarters of the way.

It would have been rude for me to refuse the plate, but
I didn't want to waste any talk time, smile time, laugh time.
The early stage of flirtation demands complete attention; it
can't be diverted by English trifles. But Julian insisted, and
the guys kept telling me which dessert I should try first, so I
grabbed an enormous strawberry. It was far too big for one bite,
so I started licking away at the white chocolate peak: casual,
deliberate, unhurried licks. Next I nibbled just a second or two,
delicately, around the stem. Then I smiled (knowingly) and bit
(thoroughly) into the ripe red strawberry flesh. A droplet or two
of nectar ran down my bottom lip, and I didn't wipe it off until
I felt sure that my intentions were as transparent as my green
silk shirt.

There's a fine line between almost manic and mostly

manic, when charmingly indiscreet turns into just plain indiscreet, and seductive becomes obnoxious. For me, that line always gets fainter and fuzzier the closer I get to mania, until eventually there is no line, there never was a line, and any line that might have been disappears altogether, along with all of my discretion and judgment.

The angle of the sun had changed since I'd entered Julian's house. Midday had mellowed to early evening, but I could still see the line there in Julian's kitchen. True, the damn thing kept moving on me, but I could still see it. I knew it was there. I knew that my little strip-tease act with the strawberry had come perilously close to the edge; and that any more foreplay with my desserts would surely push me over.

I had to shift the focus, fast. There's no telling what manic lips might say, although you can be sure it will be laced with profanity and innuendo. I didn't know any of these men well enough to be vulgar in their presence. So no more nibbling; no more licking; no more lip action, period. I pushed my plate away with a big stage sigh, tossed my napkin on top and declared I couldn't possibly take another bite. Which naturally didn't help at all because then the word *bite* hovered over our table. There was only one thing to do: I had to shut up altogether.

Anyone who lives on the sane side of mania can't possibly imagine the agony of enforced silence. The urge to talk gets greater and greater as you head up the mood scale, until finally it's as irresistible as a sneeze in a dust storm. The clinical term for this is "pressured speech." "Pressure-cooker speech" is more like it, because unless all those unspoken words are somehow released, silence explodes into screams; and screams are not so easily ignored.

I've seen manic people use all sorts of creative ways to divert the pressure to speak. Leg jiggling is by far the favorite technique. I guarantee that in a roomful of ten manic-depressives, at least two of them will be madly jiggling away. Then there's the compulsive yawners, the twitchers, and the tappers, who will tap on anything within reach—the chair, the wall, even the person sitting next to them. I particularly admire the people who manage to talk without ever making a sound. They just form the words on their lips and chew.

My personal trick is fist-clenching. I press my nails into my palms over and over, as fast and as hard as I can, until my skin is pockmarked with gouges—deep red crescent moons that will eventually fade, but hurt like hell at the time. Pain is always a useful distraction, but any kind of rhythmic movement seems to ease the need to talk.

Little did Julian know how much he had helped by seating me on a stool that swiveled. I just love swivel chairs when I'm getting manic. I can whip back and forth and all the way around if I need to, and it almost absorbs the excess energy that would otherwise come out of my mouth.

I calculated the odds before me. Three complete spins were about all I could safely insert into the conversation without appearing bizarre or intoxicated. I took a deep breath, held it, then spun away: once around, twice around and by the third revolution I had lost most of the urge to talk. It was all I could do to stay upright on my chair. To my complete surprise, the men had continued right on talking without me.

They talked about Shaquille O'Neal and silicone lawsuits and Julian's new Mercedes. I had lots to say on all of these subjects, but I just swiveled back and forth instead: little half swivels, not so much that you'd notice, just enough to release a little pressure.

I actually stopped talking. I actually listened. So I knew that I wasn't all the way manic, because when you're all the way manic you never listen to anybody but yourself. I was maybe three-quarters of the way up, I figured, where the urges are sometimes negotiable and swivel chairs can still make a difference. At three-quarters up, my mind is running fast, but not so fast that I can't, with an intense effort, shut up and listen. But I listen with triple the intensity of normal people. I practically suck the thoughts from their brains. By the time the words are finally out of their slow, sane mouths, I not only know what they mean better than they do, I'm ten questions ahead.

I'll never know what my next move would have been that afternoon—if I would have just sat there, smiling and swiveling as the men talked on without me; or if I would have burst out into a frenzy of flirtation. I'll never know because Julian's alarm clock suddenly went off and he dashed out of the kitchen. And then I heard it—that sound, the one against which all women, however sexy or pretty or willing, are powerless: Chick Hearn announcing the Lakers pregame show.

A couple of the men paused long enough to grab a brownie and say good-bye. Then I found myself sitting all alone at the center island. All alone, with no one to charm, and worst of all, no one to talk to. Sure, I could swivel all the way around now, but what was the point of struggling to keep quiet when there was no conversation to interrupt?

The kitchen was dark now, and I realized that I wasn't alone. There were voices coming from a little alcove on the other side of the room, voices that I hadn't noticed while I was preoccupied with the men. High-pitched and overlapping, punctuated by bursts of squeaky, giggly laughter. I'd completely forgotten: the other women.

I had to do something. I couldn't just sit there spinning until the Lakers game was over. It was a difficult choice: whether to join the men, knowing that I would be ignored for the next few hours; or join the other women, knowing that I was three-quarters manic. In my case, other women and mania are incompatible. At some point on my way up the mood scale, seduction becomes my primary purpose and other women are the enemy. Old women, young women, beautiful, ugly, scrawny, curvaceous—it doesn't matter. Other women violate my fundamental right to be the only woman in the room.

But at least women talk. All women talk. So I took a last few spins on the swivel chair, and headed across the room toward the enemy camp. There were six of them, in varying degrees of pretty: three brunettes and two blondes and one sort of in-between. One of these, I knew, had to be the woman in charge, the woman I would have to cozy up to for the next several hours, or at least until the Lakers game was over and Julian was free again. And then it hit me. There was a very good chance that the woman in charge might also be *Julian's* woman.

My morality, like my memory, gets increasingly fungible the closer I get to mania. So what if Julian already had a girl?

I wasn't trespassing here, I was invited, by the greenest pair of eyes I'd seen in years. It's a well-known fact that God makes green-eyed men for one purpose only: to remind me that love is a chemical imbalance, too. That perilous highs and desperate lows and extravagant flurries of mood are not always symptoms of a broken mind, but signs of a beating heart.

If nothing else, my fourteen years as a litigator had taught me how to walk into almost any adversarial situation without showing fear. No matter how hard my heart is pounding, I can almost always extend a hand that's cool and steady, and briskly state my name in a voice that doesn't quiver. "It's just opening argument," I reminded myself as I walked up to the women's table and put a tentative hand on one of the empty chairs.

One of the blondes saw me and waved me over. She was the younger, prettier one with the pricey hair extensions: a good bet for Julian's girl, I thought. And sure enough, her tone was just a bit overeager when she turned to me and asked, "So you're a friend of Julian's?"

"We're neighbors," I replied, then, "And how long have you known Julian?" But the blonde's attention had been diverted, and I was left with nothing to do but smile into the empty air. So I listened. I quickly learned where to get the best bikini wax in Aspen; which private schools are really, truly private; and how to deduct at least half a tummy tuck from my taxes, before the pretty blonde turned back my way and said, "Some of us were wondering—we've got a bet going on, in fact—who does your color?"

Finally, I thought. A topic I could ace. Like all true redheads, I'm rather vain about my hair. I figure God would

not have made me so conspicuous if he wanted me humble.
So I grinned back at the blonde, and replied, "Actually, nobody
does my color. It's natural."

"Natural. Really?"

"Really."

"Not even highlights?"

"Never."

"How extraordinary," she said. Not "How lovely," or
"How lucky for you," or anything else that might have easily
translated into a compliment. Then she smiled at me, sweet as
a lemon tart, and said, "I think we require proof," while the rest
of the table burst into giggles.

"Well, there's only one surefire way for a redhead to prove
that she's . . ." and I faltered, then blushed to the roots of my
suspect hair. If only this table was filled with men, I thought.
Then this whole conversation would have been deliciously
naughty, and I would have been completely in control.
But mania distorts everything when women are around. It
sabotages my senses, so all I can see are arched eyebrows and
all I can hear are sneers where none, most probably, exist.
Then again, maybe they do. I never know for certain, and it's
the not knowing that drives me mad.

I needed air. I needed space. The heightened sensuality
that I had prized so much an hour before, when I was flirting
with the men, was no longer titillating; it was torture. I could
feel every rung of the hardbacked chair as it pressed up against
the small of my back, sharp and unforgiving, while all around
me the women's voices crackled like a summer storm. Nannies
was the subject now. Nannies who never showed up on time.

Nannies who wanted too much money. Seductive nannies, nannies who tried to steal the silver. The search for the perfect nanny.

The urge to talk, to interact, was still strong upon me, and I longed to join the conversation. So I thought about nannies, thought hard. I strained my memory for nanny anecdotes. Nothing came to mind. I had nothing to say.

It wasn't possible. My manic persona has a great many voices, but none of them is silent. And yet, my tongue lay slack and heavy in my mouth. I didn't care if the nannies stole all the silver. I didn't care if the Mercedes handled better than the Porsche, or which dermatologists made house calls at night, or how many pounds of carry-on luggage the Concorde allows. I thought of the mounds of bills piled high on my own kitchen table: doctors, hospitals, pharmacies, insurance, all the shrill, nagging reminders of my mental illness that I faced each morning over cold cereal and coffee. The search for a perfect nanny seemed absurdly easy somehow, in comparison to the search for sanity. Now *there* was a topic worthy of discussion.

But the room was whirling too fast for me now, too many names I didn't recognize and places I'd never been and problems I wasn't rich enough to afford. I could barely trace the outline of the huge oak tree that grew just outside the kitchen window. Some of its branches, I knew, reached all the way down into my own backyard, but they were hidden from my sight by the darkness and the angle. It would be quiet over there, I thought. Blissfully so, now that the drums had stopped. There would be no twittering voices, no faint, fragrant subtleties to provoke and confuse me. The only other woman was the one that I might, or might not, choose to see in the mirror. Strange, but the option of leaving had not occurred to me before, not while Julian, or the promise of Julian, still lingered in the vicinity. But all at once I knew: it was time to go home.

I stood up abruptly and told the blonde, "I'm sorry, but I have to leave now—I'm expecting a call."

"At least have some dessert before you go," she said, pushing a plate in my direction. "Here, take some strawberries. They're awesome."

"I know they are. But I think I've already had more strawberries than is good for me today." I turned and walked away. And I kept on walking, across the kitchen, through the foyer, and out the front door. I hesitated briefly when I reached the front gate, remembering his laughter; remembering his eyes. But I shook my head and kept right on walking, through the gate, down the street, and all the way up to my own front door. And I didn't really breathe freely again until I heard it lock safely behind me.

Then, at last, came the quiet. Thick, womblike quiet, wrapped all around me. It was just what I'd wanted—or was it? The silence magnified every sound: my heartbeat throbbed in my ears; I could almost hear my blood squeezing in and out of my capillaries. But mostly, I could hear a whiny voice in my head, asking me over and over again: "How could you leave without saying good-bye?"

I knew the answer to that question, but I didn't want to hear it. The truth is that I had to leave, because in the state I was in I never would have settled for a mere good-bye. I would have insisted on exchanging numbers with Julian, or arranging to get together again sometime soon. And I simply had no business doing that—not now, not like this, not when I was so unstable. I thought back over the day. From the moment I awoke, and every minute thereafter, I had been a quivering mass of volatility: up, down, irate, flirtatious, contentious, giddy, seductive, paranoid. I'd assumed half a dozen different personalities between daybreak and dusk. No wonder I was so tired.

I went into the bathroom, undressed, and methodically removed all my makeup. The face in the mirror was pale and quiet. You could never imagine it teasing a strawberry into submission, much less flirting with six different men at once. Freshly scrubbed and shiny, it looked like—well, like the girl next door. Which was just how I wanted Julian to think of me. It was all I'd ever really wanted, in fact: to be somebody's girl next door.

The girl next door isn't crazy. She may have her quirks, but at heart she's an innocent, simple and pure. Life touches her lightly; it doesn't leave scars. But instability like mine needs considerable distance to pass for mere quirkiness. A next-door neighbor would be much too keen a witness. He was certain to see through all my best disguises by sheer proximity. So there was no way I could risk getting any closer to Julian. He was far too close already.

I shut off the light and got into bed. It was quiet, so quiet I could hear the clock in the next room ticking, so quiet I could hear a faint whisper of hope. Nothing's impossible in the dark and the quiet. If I've learned anything from life as a manic-depressive, it's that things never stay the same for very long. The cruelest curse of the disease is also its most sacred promise: You will not feel this way forever.

I closed my eyes and pictured myself walking up to Julian's front gate in my prettiest peach cashmere sweater, hair tied back with a satin ribbon, a girl-next-door glow on my face. I knew it would never happen, of course, because dreams are one thing and manic depression is another. But I let myself slide off to sleep anyway, believing—just this once—in maybe.

6

The room was a cheery one, as institutions go: daisies on the wallpaper, canary yellow sheets. It looked just like a first-class spa—which it ought to, at those prices. My insurance wasn't going to cover it, but that was nothing new. This was back before any kind of mental health coverage had gone into effect. Care of the psyche was considered elective, on a par with plastic surgery.

Even if insurance had covered my stay, it wouldn't have mattered. I was so afraid that my employer would find out the truth about me, I never submitted any bills. It was early in my career, and I was still angling to land a big case. So no one at the law firm even knew I was in therapy. My cover? Ongoing dental problems that forced my absence from the office for a couple of hours each week.

Perhaps I was being too cautious. My firm, after all, was one of the most liberal in Beverly Hills, famous for espousing humanitarian causes, for championing the rights of the poor and the weak. But weakness in a client is one thing; weakness in a lawyer is something else altogether. In my second year, all the junior associates were given hand-tooled leather copies of *The Art of War* for Hanukkah, because that was how we saw ourselves, as modern-day warriors, and warriors are never allowed to be weak.

So I slunk in and out of my therapist's office. I knew that I needed to be there, but I didn't quite know why. I had no official diagnosis. All I knew was that something was wrong, terribly wrong, and had been for almost a year. My body wouldn't move. Every gesture felt leaden and labored. Even breathing required an effort of will. Worst of all, I couldn't answer the phone. The message slips kept piling up and up until stacks of little white papers littered my desk. And yet, I somehow managed to keep my job. Unhappiness in a lawyer seemed to be the norm, nothing worth getting upset about.

My therapist acknowledged the demands of my practice, but that was only a part of it, he said. There was more to my misery than met the eye. Just what, he didn't know or tell me. But every Monday and Thursday, he would sit in his big brown swivel-back chair and nod as I cried my way through half a box of tissues. After a while I almost forgot he was there. I left reality behind in the waiting room and began to speak my fantasies out loud: how I wished everyone in my law firm would die and leave me, at last, alone, or how I wished I could fall asleep one night and never wake up.

Finally, he spoke. "Personally, I hate ultimatums. But professionally, I feel I have no choice but to tell you that unless you agree to be hospitalized, I will be forced to commit you myself."

"You—you're kidding, right?"

He shook his head. "I couldn't be more serious. For three months now, I've listened to you talk about death as if it was some kind of romantic adventure. That's simply not normal cognition."

"But it's not supposed to be normal," I said. "I was just fantasizing—no, free-associating would be a better term. That's what you're supposed to do in a therapist's office, right? Free-associate?"

He leaned back in his chair. "Your fantasies are the key to your subconscious," he said. "And your subconscious obviously wants to die."

"But I *can't* go to the hospital," I said with frustration. "I've got an appellate brief due at the end of the month, and three motions in limine next week."

To my surprise, he said, "I'll tell you what I'll do. If you promise to check yourself in voluntarily, you can leave whenever you like."

"What kind of hospital are we talking about?"

"There's a very nice place not far from here. Exclusive, quiet, beautiful grounds."

"And what would I be expected to do if I went there?"

"Whatever you like. Read, rest, putter around in the

garden. We've come a long way since *The Snake Pit*, you know."

"But it's still a mental hospital—won't there be a lot of lunatics there?"

He smiled. "Come on, you ought to know better than that. Rich people are never crazy, they're colorful. And it ought to be a healthy change for you, after being surrounded by lawyers all day. Maybe it would help if you thought of it this way. Your brain is like a Ferrari—it's a world-class instrument when it's running right. But it's highly temperamental, and sometimes it needs a good tune-up. You wouldn't take a Ferrari in to a Jiffy Lube to get serviced, would you? No, you'd take it in to the Ferrari shop, and let the experts tinker away. Let's let the experts take a look at you."

How well he knew me. It was not for nothing that of all the towns in all the world, I had settled in Beverly Hills. Nor was it any great surprise that I had insisted on a first-rate education. I knew the truth: snobbery was part of my character. I wanted—no, I expected—the best. Not out of a sense of entitlement, though. I thought of it as self-protection. For as long as I could remember, I had always been far too sensitive to my surroundings. Dirt and squalor made me physically ill, even if I was simply watching it on TV. If money could not buy happiness, at least it could buy harmony. Simply by wielding a credit card, I could manipulate the surface of things— substitute symmetry for dissonance, balance for distortion.

I took refuge in aesthetics. I hoped, in fooling my eye, to fool myself as well; and quite often, I succeeded. Better yet, I learned to fool the world by letting my possessions speak up for me. As in, I am successful enough to own a Porsche: I must be well-adjusted. Or, Look at my Armani suit: how well my life must fit me.

So the Ferrari analogy hit home. Maybe that was exactly what I needed—a little fine-tuning at the cautious hands of experts. "How much would three days cost me?" I asked, and my therapist quoted a ridiculous sum. And yet, it was the price that cinched it. I figured anything that cost that much must be the best. Plus it must be beautiful, the sort of thick-wall-against-the-world kind of beauty that keeps ugliness from seeping in.

I took three days off work the next week by claiming a death in the family. I actually felt surprisingly good driving there with the late-afternoon sun streaming through the windows. The only thing that was really bothering me was how I'd packed: hastily, at the last moment, and in considerable confusion. What do you wear to a loony bin? Coco Chanel, who had something to say on everything, was silent on this.

The sign to Casa Pacifica was so discreet I almost missed it. I made a quick right turn onto a graveled road marked Private Access Only. I liked the sound of that. At the end of the bougainvillea path was a large, white-shuttered building, in front of which grew the biggest weeping willow tree that I had ever seen. A swarm of attendants came out to meet me. They were not, I was relieved to see, wearing institution white, but rather a gentle shade of blue that reminded me, quite pleasantly, of the ten-milligram dose of Valium. One took my bags, one took my car, and a third, a tall, patrician-looking lady with good teeth and white hair, smiled and held out her hand. "Welcome to Casa Pacifica," she said. "Come on, let's get you settled."

I followed her into a cozy lobby all decked out in chintz and flowers. Casablanca lilies, my all-time favorites. I stopped in front of one and inhaled. The woman said, "You're a fan of Casablancas?" I nodded. "We can have some sent to your room, if you like." I nodded again. I wasn't ready to let my guard down yet, although from everything I'd seen so far, this place might just turn out all right.

Half an hour later, I was sitting in the woman's office having tea and biscuits while she went over the rules. All two of them. "You must meet with a therapist once a day. And you have to keep a journal." Neither sounded onerous, and then came the kicker: "I hope you'll be all right on your own. It will just be for one night. Your roommate isn't expected until tomorrow."

Roommate? What roommate? I'd never had a roommate in my life, not even in college, and I certainly didn't intend to start now. Roommates could be messy and noisy and ugly, and you couldn't control them, not even with a credit card. I explained to the woman, softly but emphatically, that I preferred to be alone, that I'd be happy to pay a premium if that's what it took to get a single room. She smiled at me and shook her head. "I'm sorry, dear, but everyone here at Casa Pacifica is expected to have a roommate. We consider it therapeutic."

Mistaking my silence for acquiescence, she offered to show me my room. In spite of all my misgivings, I couldn't help but be charmed by the slanting roof, the huge bay window and the daisies in a blue Delft vase on the bedside table. The sun was just beginning to set, and the room glowed yellow and white.

It wasn't until I knelt down on the window seat to look at the view that I noticed the fine mesh steel on the windows.

"These windows don't open, do they?" I asked.

"Well, no, not really. You have to have a key."

"Speaking of which, no one has given me a room key yet."

"You don't need a key. The staff will lock things up at night, so you don't have to do a thing."

"You mean the staff will lock *me* up at night, don't you?"

"Technically, yes. But it's just for your protection."

I wanted to be left alone, so I dropped it. I thanked the woman for all her help, and told her I wanted to take a stroll around the grounds.

"Just so you know, the gardens close at dusk."

She left. I rifled through my suitcase for a sweater, then headed outside. Part of me was already starting to panic at the thought of being locked in for the night, but I breathed easier once I was outdoors. The sun was setting in earnest by then, so I sat down in a thick patch of grass and rolled onto my back. God was painting with the big box of crayons, and beauty, as always, worked its magic on me. I forgot who I was, where I was, how I got there. It wasn't until I noticed a pale crescent moon in the corner of the sky that I remembered that I had to be back by dusk. Which meant I really ought to get up and get going.

My body rebelled against the thought. "You are not bound by such rules. They're intended strictly for the mental patients, and to be a mental patient, you first have got to be mentally ill. And you are most certainly, categorically, *not* mentally ill." How could I be? I, who was voted Most Likely to Succeed, who graduated Vassar College with honors and represented major moguls and movie stars—how could I be crazy? Crazy people acted strange. When they spoke, their words betrayed them. Whereas I used words as weapons. No one would ever think, to look at me, that I spent so much of my time either holding back tears or engulfed in them. But still, that wasn't mental illness. That was plain old-fashioned misery. The wrong profession, a lackluster love life, a chronic lack of sleep. . .

I ran back toward the building, stumbling across the uneven grass. I paused just out of sight of the lobby to shake the hair out of my eyes and freshen the crease in my pants. Further proof that I was sane, I thought. Crazy people are frayed at the seams. I needn't have bothered: no one was there. At dinner, perhaps. I had no interest in food. Not food per se, but the drudgery of picking it out and cutting it up and lifting it over and over again from fork to mouth to fork to mouth to fork to mouth and so on. Life was already far too full of mindless repetitions, like the endless droning monotony of drawing breath or pumping blood. It seemed like such a waste of time. One breath, one beat, was just the same as any other. Air was air and blood was blood and no matter what you ate for dinner, it all wound up as shit.

When I got to my room, to my surprise, the air was suddenly rich and sweet. The daisies had been replaced by a huge ceramic pitcher filled with Casablanca lilies. They were so beautiful, I knew that nothing very horrible could happen in their presence. I lay down and closed my eyes.

Eight hours later, I woke to a knock at the door, reminding me, "Therapy in fifteen minutes!" I kicked myself free of the canary yellow sheets and ran to the bathroom, brushed my teeth, dragged a comb through my hair and slipped into a pair of neatly pressed jeans.

When I opened the door, an attendant was there, waiting to escort me. "You'll like Dr. Han," he said, leading me down a long series of halls. "He's one of our best." Best. Not the word I would have used to describe him. Everything about the man was gray: from his snagged and rumpled cardigan to the circles underneath his eyes to the salt-and-pepper hair combed carefully across his head. Even his voice sounded gray when he told me to sit down, we were going to take some tests. He asked me to fill in the captions for a collection of outlandish cartoons. Then he asked me to finish a series of statements with the very first answer that popped in my head. A typical exchange:

Q. "If I could be anything in the world, then I would be . . ."
A. "Invisible."
Q. "If I could do anything that I liked, then I would . . ."
A. "Disappear."

I must admit, I was actually enjoying myself. I've always enjoyed taking tests, not for the sake of the tests themselves, but for the glory of the good grade afterward. So when I asked Dr. Han how I did, I expected what I had heard most of my life: praise. Instead, he said: "These really aren't that kind of test. They're not like, say, the SATs."

Bullshit, I thought. Everything, up to and including life,

was exactly like the SATs: you either scored well or you didn't. But the question I really wanted to ask him was, "Do you know what's wrong with me?" Although the words were tugging at my tongue, I couldn't set them free. Just seven simple words, but I was afraid the silence afterward would stretch into eternity. Or else—God forbid—he'd actually have an answer.

Dr. Han stood up and clapped me on the back. "I know just what you need," he said. I looked at him, expectantly. "A good hot cup of soup."

I followed him as he led me back through the maze of halls to the dining room, where he left me. There were a dozen or so people gathered there, mostly at one table. At first I thought they might be staff. They looked decidedly normal to me: laughing, chatting, eating their food. But as I looked a little bit closer I noticed one woman was actually attacking her steak, sawing at it savagely, as if it might be still alive. A fat young man in khaki shorts was jiggling all over, legs and arms and double chins all independently a-tremble. And three or four of the rest of them kept wiping their mouths to dislodge, I noticed with a sudden shudder, quite copious amounts of drool.

I grabbed my journal and retraced my steps toward the garden. I flopped down and began to sketch. Nothing was as I remembered it, though. The clouds, so fine and wispy the day before, had grown thick and gray, obscuring the sun. Drops began to splash down onto my page. The sky had betrayed me: it was no longer shelter. I buttoned up my sweater and got to my feet.

When I reached my room, I was thoroughly wet and longing for my lilies. But something was standing between me and them—a figure, human enough until it turned around. I gasped. Her face was a patchwork of scarlet and white, shiny in some spots and mottled in others. Her features on one side had melted and blurred. Her left arm was a stump, although her right was intact, still freckled and fair. She looked at me, then turned away.

I cursed myself for that embarrassing gasp. As a lawyer, I was trained to keep my feelings under wraps. I held out my hand. "You must be my new roommate," I said, and I hoped my smile hid my trembling. Part of me was downright scared, part of me was furious, not with the poor woman in front of me but with the institution. They should have prepared me for this.

She mumbled her name, then got into bed. Her face was hidden in the pillow, but I could tell by the shuddering of her shoulders that she was crying. I thought longingly of the garden I had just left, the wide-open expanse that made no demands of me. Fighting the urge to throw open the door, I crossed the room and stood over the bed.

"I'm sorry, did you say something?" I asked.

"Wish I was invisible," a quivering voice replied. "Wish I could just disappear."

I was utterly unnerved. I recognized her language. It was the language of suffering, and I knew it well. We were one and the same, the girl and I. The only difference was that my scars were on the inside, where they didn't show.

The instinctive aversion to her appearance was drowned out by a sudden flood of empathy, and to my surprise, I reached down and gathered her up in my arms. Her skin felt

thin and wrinkled, like crumpled tissue paper. At first she tried
to pull away, but I hushed her and started stroking her hair,
rocking her back and forth in my arms.

Her long blond hair was healthy, luxurious even, in my
hands. I wondered at the irony of this ornamentation: of what
possible use was such hair to her now? But beauty, true beauty,
is never wasted. In fact, her hair was all the more glorious
because of the contrast with her damaged skin.

And that's when it hit me: I had been going about it all
wrong. It was futile to try to deny the existence of ugliness—
either in the world, or in myself. God made light, and God
made monsters, and there must have been a reason for that.
As Saint Augustine said, "Even monsters are divine creatures
and in some way they too belong to the providential order
of nature." Without the darkness, how can we ever hope to
understand the light?

I started to cry. True beauty, I realized, is not the absence of
ugliness, but the acceptance of it. And I knew then what I had
refused to admit all along: that I was indeed mentally ill.

I welcomed the monster. I gave it a home.

It was March 22. I remember the date because, every
year, I send an anonymous card to Phoebe, for that was the
young girl's name. It's a simple card. There are only two words
printed on it: "Thank you." I send it anonymously because
I don't know how to explain. I only know that my greatest
victories have always been surrenders.

7

We were the Gatsby couple, or so our friends
called us. We made a martini look good. It was the eighties,
and he was as essential to me as shoulder pads. His intellect
gave me breadth; his beauty gave me symmetry. I was never so
complete as when I stepped into a crowded room as his other
half.

But bipolar disorder always chooses the most inopportune
times to remind you that remission is just a respite, not a cure.
I'd had several bad episodes of both mania and depression
while Rick and I were seeing each other, back when I was in
college and law school. To his credit, he had been kind and
gentle, if a bit bewildered by it all. But then all at once the

floodgates broke loose, and a depression of biblical savagery swept over me. I could barely move, let alone make it to class. What little energy I had was devoted to deceiving the people around me into believing that I simply had a lingering case of the flu. I had neither the time nor the inclination for romance. The care and feeding of a lover was completely beyond my capabilities.

I knew that I was losing Rick. Our phone calls became fewer and shorter each night, until they basically consisted of the same three sentences: "Any better?" "No." "That's a shame." It *was* a shame, a damned shame, but the breakup wasn't the worst of it all. What really tortured me were the dreams that visited me night after night, when I would remember in full sensory detail the exact expression of Rick's gray-green eyes when he told me I was beautiful; the timbre of his voice when he called me sweetheart; and his sigh when he held me in his arms after making love. The memory of sustenance is a terrible thing. Far worse, I think, than actual starving. Starving just kills you. Longing can gnaw away at you forever.

But Rick was a rescuer, and I hadn't been properly rescued yet, although I was getting tremendous help from a new medication regime. The drugs knocked the depression to its knees, but they kept me just this side of manic. So the next time I saw Rick, several years later, I was definitely high—not so high that I looked or acted inappropriate, but high enough that I sparkled, I glittered, I was as charming as the quicksilver moon.

I ran into Rick again while I was waiting for my car outside a fashionable restaurant, the kind of L.A. hot spot that we used to frequent together in our Jay and Daisy era. I was a full-fledged entertainment lawyer by then, and my job required me to waste a lot of time in such places. I remember I was feeling chilly and bored that night, and my feet hurt. I was standing alone by the door, looking for the valet, when a red Lamborghini roared up to the portico. Ever since I was given a 1965 Corvette for my sixteenth birthday, I've been a sucker for sports cars, and this one was a full-throttle work of art. I let out an involuntary "Wow!" and heard a familiar voice behind me say, "Thank you." Sure enough, it was Rick, looking every bit as handsome and sexy as I remembered him.

We started talking so fast we were almost talking over each other: me, because I was practically manic, and Rick because I think he was genuinely glad to see me. The Lamborghini turned out to be his reward for selling a screenplay. I was so proud of him, I started to cry. Just like old times, I thought, except now they were actually tears of joy.

After fifteen minutes of catching up, Rick said, "It's a beautiful night. Why don't we go for a drive?" and our relationship took off again from there. He careened up Benedict Canyon Drive with one eye on the road and the other on me. "I can't get over how good you look," he kept saying. "It's like the old you, come back to life."

I was perfectly happy to be the old me, especially when we parked on Mulholland Drive and looked out at the sparkling city below. "It's your town," I whispered to Rick, and before I knew it his arm was around me and he was kissing me again, with lips that still remembered every curve and nuance of my own. And I was kissing him back.

We saw each other the next night, and the next, and the night after that. At that point, Rick told me the truth: he was living with someone. "It's a rotten relationship, and I'm not in love anymore," he confessed. "But she needs me—she's had a rough life, and I'm the only thing she's got." I was devastated, but incipient mania got in the way of my better judgment. I didn't stop to ask myself whether I should be in this relationship at all. I only asked myself how I could manage to stay. I was determined to pummel the relationship into submission. Either that, or pretend there was no problem at all.

Pretending worked pretty well for a while. For the next six months, we saw each other several nights a week. Rick's girlfriend either didn't care very much, or she didn't expect to know where he was. Then one night, long after I'd gone to sleep, Rick called me and said, "Sarah's going to see her sister in Connecticut this weekend. It's our chance to finally get out of town. What do you say to La Valencia?" He knew how I loved La Valencia Hotel—a little pink paradise just north of San Diego, in the immaculate seaside village of La Jolla.

Much as I loved La Jolla, I didn't say yes immediately. The increasing volatility of my mood had been bothering me. I was no longer reliably three-quarters manic. When I was under too much stress, particularly deadlines, I began to plummet into something that resembled depression. It wasn't full-blown depression, but it was close enough to make me nervous about going away. My mooring lines had slipped. I wasn't quite sure in which direction I might suddenly find myself headed.

I tried to explain all this to Rick, but he was having none

of it. "I've never seen you so stable," he kept reassuring me. Rick could sell sand in the desert, so it didn't take long before I finally agreed. I packed for emergencies.

We took off late that Friday afternoon, and arrived at the hotel just as the sun went down. Rick had a craving for abalone and went to talk to the concierge about restaurants. I was sticky and tired after the long drive, so I ran a warm bubble bath in the Jacuzzi tub, and sank down to my shoulders in lavender-scented bliss. But the second I closed my eyes, thoughts started swarming my brain: this isn't right, I shouldn't be here, this is stolen time. I didn't know Rick's girlfriend, Sarah, but by all rights these were her lavender bubbles, this was her tub, and that was her man coming through the door, whistling "There's a Small Hotel."

"We're all set," Rick said. "The finest seafood restaurant in La Jolla, and it's only a few blocks away. The concierge said to dress." That meant that for the next few hours, my mind would be preoccupied with other things, deeply important things like mousse and mascara and the line of a black seamed stocking. I'd brought my very favorite evening dress along: a complicated wasp-waisted, full-skirted affair with honest-to-God petticoats. Rick was all smiles when he saw me dressed for dinner. "You look like Grace Kelly in *Rear Window*," he said.

Guilt is a rotten thing for the digestion. The abalone was fresh and in season, but I couldn't taste it. The Bach, the candles, the white-jacketed waiter, all of it was wasted on me. By the time the strawberry tartlets arrived, I couldn't stand it anymore. I had to speak.

"Rick, we have to talk about Sarah," I said. "What are you

planning to do about her? Do you ever intend to tell her about us? In fact, is there any 'us' to tell her about?"

Rick put his fork down and looked at me, annoyance showing on his face. "Of course there's an 'us.' What do you think we've been doing all these months?"

"That's my question. What *have* we been doing all these months?"

"I think what we have is very special," he said. "Can't we just leave it at that?"

Luckily for him, the waiter came by at that moment to ask monsieur if he would care for a cigar. Rick was brave: he opted to stretch out the meal, or maybe he just didn't want to be alone with me yet. In any event, he said yes. I was glad. I wanted to make up for the tension between us, and a surefire way of pleasing Rick was to go through what we called the *Gigi* routine: I chose his cigar by holding it up to my ear and rolling it between my fingertips; then I cut the tip and lit the match while he puffed away. Normally I find this a very soothing routine. I like being old-fashioned and submissive— as long as it's understood that it's only a routine.

But that night, the ritual only inflamed my mood. The flare of the match head startled me. I couldn't tear my eyes away from the flame, which could only mean one thing: I was manic. I have a fascination with all things incendiary when I'm manic. I surround myself with candles; I cultivate friends with fireplaces; and I simply love to watch things burn. I'll stand for hours, plucking strands of hair from my head and tossing them onto the stove just to see them sizzle. That night

I stared so long into the flame that Rick had to reach out and snatch the match from my hand.

"What's the matter with you?" he said.

"It's because of the manic depression, isn't it?" I said.

He glanced away, just for a second. "The truth is, you seem so much better these days, like a whole different person," he said. "But. . . ."

"But?"

"But I'm still waiting to see if it's real."

When you're manic, your mind is running so fast that you can easily envision alternate endings to any given moment. So I could see myself standing up and storming out of the restaurant. I could see myself sitting quietly and smiling rather sadly. And I could see myself thrusting my hand into the candle flame and saying, "You want real? I'll show you real."

Although I wanted a dramatic release, I settled for the Mona Lisa smile. My mind had already jumped ten steps ahead: if I could just fool Rick into thinking everything was okay, maybe I could convince him to let me go for a walk alone after we left the restaurant. I knew that I couldn't face a hotel bed, not now, not with his rejection still quivering between us.

After the check came, I told Rick that I was going to take a quick walk along the park between our hotel and the sea. "It's after eleven," he said. "I'll be just a few steps away," I reassured him. "Besides, the park is well patrolled." All of La Jolla is well patrolled. He reluctantly agreed, as long as I was back before midnight.

I knew exactly where I wanted to go. Across the park was a series of steps that led directly down to a cove, protected on all three sides by sheer rock. I wanted to feel the cool, wet sand against my feet, so I kicked off my heels, and made my way across the stretch of grass that separates La Jolla proper from the sea.

"Do Not Enter. Danger. Riptide" read the wooden sign at the top of the steps. No one was around. I ducked under the chain, past the sign and down the mist-slick steps to the beach. Maintaining my balance was a constant struggle. I was finally forced to stop at one point and remove my panty hose. I left them on a nearby outcropping of rock, then I continued all the way down to the beach.

It was just as I had remembered it: vicious, lonely, the kind of place where pirates would have hidden their treasure or ravished their maidens. There was only a tiny strip of sand to stand on, and even from there, it was impossible not to get wet. It looked like the tide was rising; but what did I care, I was here. I stepped into the freezing water. Within minutes, my feet were completely numb. I didn't notice the cold anymore. I didn't even notice the wet. My feet had completely ceased to exist.

What if? a voice in my head kept asking, tugging at me like the tide. What if all of you were blessedly numb? What if your mind didn't always think, think, think?

I looked up at the sky. It was a clear, starry night, with an exquisite Van Gogh kind of brilliance. Well, I was sick of the exquisite brilliance of madness. I wanted simple and sane. Barring that, I wanted nothing. I wanted numb. Lifting my petticoats as high as I could, I stepped in further and let the water wash over my knees and thighs. The pain was searing. I forced myself to stand rock still until the pain gave way to nothing at all.

What if? I slipped my dress up over my head and threw it onto the rocks. I slipped off my bra and panties, too, and flung them up there as well. Naked, I stepped into the surf.

Crash! A wave assaulted me from the left. I staggered, slipped, then found my footing. Crash! Another wave hit me from the right, knocking me off balance and sending me into the water. It wouldn't be long until I was thoroughly numb. I just had to stay upright long enough to let the cold work its way through me.

It never even occurred to me just to lie back and let the water have its way with me. That would have been suicide, and I didn't necessarily want to be dead, just dormant for a while. I had to escape. Manic feelings are sometimes so brutally strong it seems like there is no way to endure them. To me, there was nothing crazy about immersing myself in a freezing riptide at a quarter till midnight. Crazy would have been continuing to feel the way I did.

So we danced together, the tide and I. I began to relax into the ocean's rhythm: the boom-and-swish, boom-and-swish percussion of the waves. My eyelids grew heavy, and a drowsy warmth began to move through my body. My head started nodding, my eyes kept closing, and I found myself slipping deeper into the tide's embrace. We danced together as one now, the only dance my body knew, the only dance I'd ever known . . . the riptide tango: three steps forward, three steps forward, two steps back.

The water was up to my chin, and I was actually starting to get scared. I wanted to go back to the strip of beach, but the little beach was no longer there. There was nothing but water now, all around me—and in the distance, on an outcropping of rock, a glimpse of my green silk evening gown, flapping wildly in the breeze.

And then the most extraordinary thing happened. The stars came loose from their moorings and started chasing one another across the sky. One by one they shot through the night, trailing arcs of shimmering silver behind them. For a brief spectacular moment, the entire sky was afire, like a giant's birthday cake. Then the sky was extinguished and the darkness reclaimed its own.

I knew there was probably a simple explanation for what I had just seen, but I didn't want to hear it. I was in the mood for messages: I wanted to believe that what had just happened meant something. I couldn't imagine what that might be. Between the surf and the chattering of my teeth, it was simply too noisy to concentrate. All I could think was, thank God I didn't blink. And maybe that was the message all along: Don't blink, never blink, or you'll miss the whole show.

That's all I had been doing: blinking. Closing my eyes to reality, refusing to see the truth about Rick and me. No wonder I'd been getting depressed again. The world was full of shooting stars, and I was settling for the blackness.

I was fully awake now and aware of the danger. I reached underwater and began rubbing my legs, rubbing my arms, rubbing all of me. Some feeling returned to my limbs, which hurt like the devil. Why, I wondered, is pain so necessary for survival? But then an enormous wave surged up and slapped me full in the face. I got the point: now was not the time to philosophize. Now, right now, was the time to survive.

I shouted for help, but there was no one to hear—and I didn't necessarily want to be heard. Men had been rescuing me all my life. For once, I wanted to rescue myself. I plunged toward the shore. I advanced a few feet, only to be sucked back out. I pushed again harder, again, and again, gaining a little more ground each time. Trembling, gagging, spitting up seawater, I finally emerged from the waves and fell onto the beach.

I lay there until my breathing slowed and my pulse returned to a regular rhythm. Then I lifted myself up and over to the rock where my dress still hung, still flapping briskly in the breeze. It took me a few tries, but I finally snared it. It was damp but wearable. I slid it over my head and smoothed it out around my hips and I was suddenly civilized again, notwithstanding my wet and dripping hair. Then carefully, I climbed my way out of the cave and up toward the park, past where my shoes lay patiently waiting, past the Danger sign.

To my shock, the clock on the lobby wall said a quarter past three. Rick would either have called the police by now or fallen asleep. I bet on the latter. Rick could fall asleep anywhere and everywhere after midnight—in a movie theater, a play, my bedroom, his car. Rather than risk waking him up, I decided to ask the desk clerk for a key. He made no comment on my bedraggled appearance. He simply handed me the key and bid me a good night.

When I opened the door, it was just as I expected: Rick was asleep, one arm flung across my side of the bed. I wondered if I'd worried him. I wondered if he'd missed me. And I wondered what I was going to say when he finally woke up.

I went into the bathroom, dried my hair with a towel, and put on a robe. I stepped out onto the terrace, sat on one of the deck chairs and heard a sound from the bedroom. I poked my head through the door. Rick was mumbling and fidgeting in his sleep. I couldn't make out what he was trying to say, but I did hear him distinctly say my name. Then he reached across the bed and grabbed the pillow, the pillow on which my head should have been laying, and he hugged it to his chest.

Did that mean he loved me in his dreams? Maybe I mattered far more than he knew; and maybe I was about to make a horrible mistake. I stepped back out onto the balcony and looked to the sky for answers. Orion had all but disappeared. I couldn't see the Big Dipper, either. In fact, I couldn't make out any of the constellations at all. The sky was haphazard and made no sense.

Nothing's colder and lonelier than a manic morning after. I'm never quite sure what actually happened, and what's just a by-product of my feverish imagination. Did the sky ever really explode with shooting stars, and if so, what did that mean? Did it mean anything at all?

I chose to let the stars decide. I would lie here and watch the sky until morning. If I saw another shooting star by then, it would mean that I was supposed to break up with Rick. If I saw nothing, then I would just let things go on between us the way they were. I settled in. I didn't have to wait long: within fifteen minutes, a flash of silver streaked through the sky. It happened so fast, the image barely registered before it was gone. Maybe I was seeing things, I thought. If I saw *two* shooting stars sometime before morning, that would clearly be a sign from God that I should end it with Rick.

Four, maybe five minutes later, another streak of silver shot through the sky. Then another. Then another. Then a sudden barrage of brilliance. Surely this was some kind of astronomical phenomenon, a once-every-blue-moon spectacle like Halley's Comet or the convergence of Venus and Mars. If so, it wasn't fair to use it to decide my fate. It wasn't normal. It wasn't natural. It was loaded dice.

Part of me protested at this. "What better evidence could you possibly want?" I asked myself. Deep down I knew I was probably right. And I also knew that there weren't enough shooting stars in the galaxy to convince me that I should break up with Rick.

There are all kinds of riptides, and love is surely the most powerful. I'd been sucked in so deep I could barely find my footing anymore. For the second time that evening, I was in danger of drowning. I was fully conscious, and I knew exactly what I was doing. I was doing the wrong thing.

I thought back to my epiphany earlier that night. "Don't blink, never blink." Manic epiphanies are like shooting stars: flashes of brilliance that are gone in an instant.

8

It's a little-known secret, and it should probably
stay that way: attempting suicide usually jump-starts your brain
chemistry. There must be something about taking all those
pills that either floods the brain sufficiently or depletes it so
completely that balance is restored. Whatever the mechanism,
the result is that you emerge on the other side of the attempt
with an awareness of what it means to be alive. Simple acts
seem miraculous: you can stand transfixed for hours just
watching the wind ruffle the tiny hairs along the top of your
arm. And always, with every sensation, is the knowledge that
you must have survived for a reason. You just can't doubt it
anymore. You must have a purpose, or you would have died.

You have the rest of your life to discover what that purpose is. And you can't wait to start looking.

My search began in Africa. I hadn't planned on going there, but then, I hadn't planned on being alive at all. In early 1991 I'd made a sincere but thwarted suicide attempt (amateurish in comparison to the attempt I would make several years later in Santa Fe). Not long afterward, a girlfriend called to ask me if I'd be interested in going on safari with her. She was supposed to go with her boyfriend, but he was having problems. She knew I was unhappy at work, wasn't a vacation just what I needed?

Lisa didn't know anything about my recent suicide attempt. No one did, except my doctors and the paramedics who had saved me. But she was right about my unhappiness. For the past two years, I had become increasingly miserable, in spite of my promotions and pay raises. The worse I felt on the inside, it seemed, the greater my success. Part of this was due, ironically, to the depression: I had to try harder than everyone else, and trying harder ultimately had its rewards. But the rest of it—the finest part—was all David's doing.

David was a senior associate in my law firm. He was one year ahead of me, my assigned professional mentor. But his protection extended well beyond the confines of our careers. I already knew that I was different. David was the first person who ever taught me that different might also mean special.

David had come out of the closet when he first started with the firm several years before, and he had braved it with an unfailing dignity and self-respect, until he was finally just "David," just one of the guys. He was the only associate in our buttoned-down, striped-tie firm to wear red silk shirts with the occasional paisley cravat. But on him, it looked great. Everything he ever wore looked great, he was gorgeous. I wouldn't say he was altogether good, and he certainly didn't like everyone, which made it so special to be one of the few who was welcome to gather in his office after hours to bitch about a nasty partner, commiserate about a stubborn judge, or, in my case, despair about life altogether.

David was the first professional colleague I ever told about my manic depression, and he took it in stride. He checked up on me whenever I didn't show up at work and never criticized me for not returning his calls. Sometimes he tucked little notes in my desk drawer or inside a file, so I got a sudden jolt of love just when I least expected it. He taught me all about tulips and burgundy wines. And most important of all, David thought I could write. He pushed me to write as a career, and damn near convinced me to do it. But then he got sick, and nothing else mattered; and nothing else would, for a very long time.

AIDS was just a scathing rumor back then—a scourge somewhere far on the other side of the world, devastating but nothing any of us need worry about. At first David's persistent coughs and headaches and assorted aches and pains yielded to medication, but inevitably came the day when the drugs stopped working. I, of course, had great empathy for this tortuous scenario, having been through my own version of it with the depression drug regime. But all at once David suddenly got much sicker, so sick he couldn't come to work anymore. The next time I saw him, a week or so later, his hair was falling out, and he was unable to eat. Over the next three weeks he stopped eating altogether, and the lithe gymnast's body became cadaverously thin, while that thick, wavy head of hair was nothing but a memory in his bedside photograph. And then his mind succumbed, and he no longer knew me; and heartless or not, I have to admit I was glad that the end came soon after that. I had never known death so intimately before.

My depression, bad enough before David's illness, tripled in intensity after his funeral. Nothing about my lifestyle, not even the large bonus I got when I was promoted into David's position, brought me any comfort. All I could think of was death. It would mean an end, at last, to this impossible façade. Plus, I figured, David would be there. I held off two weeks until David's birthday, then quickly gulped down all the pills I could get my hands on. Then I lay back on my bed and waited.

My boyfriend found me sprawled on the carpet the next morning, and the paramedics were quick on the scene. The very next day my brain chemistry kicked into overdrive and I began a brand-new love affair with life. So overwhelming was my newfound desire to experience life to its fullest that two weeks later, when Lisa asked me to go on safari, all I could think of was how wonderful! How absolutely marvelous!

You probably have to know me to know just how bizarre this is. I am not at all an outdoorsy kind of girl. I consider hailing a taxicab to count as strenuous exercise. I went camping once—when I was six years old and couldn't get out of it. Ever since, I've boycotted any activity that doesn't come with a blow dryer and might possibly involve spiders. Even so, I agreed, aware that even the most well-appointed safari would probably mean bad plumbing and bugs. Such is the power of postsuicidal euphoria: anything seems possible, even hiking boots.

So I said yes. Yes to Lisa, yes to Africa, yes to life itself.

I got stuck with a big preliminary injunction, an emergency favor for a senior partner, the week before I was supposed to leave for Kenya. I had no choice but to take it, which meant that I had to work nonstop, night and day, for five days before we took off. I wasn't worried about exhaustion. I had survived on far less sleep before. But I knew that prolonged sleep deprivation does all sorts of funny things to your brain chemistry when you're manic-depressive. Sometimes it sends you tumbling down into depression; sometimes it kicks you straight up into mania. In any event, it almost always destabilizes you in some way. Add the long flight over, the multiple time zones, and I knew I was tempting fate. I just didn't know in which direction.

I thought I would sleep on the plane, but I was too wired from both excitement and five days' worth of caffeine. Lisa slept beside me, and I wondered whether I should tell her that oh, by the way, I was manic-depressive and there was a better-than-average chance that my brain chemistry might be going slightly haywire in the very near future. But then we started our descent and the moment was gone.

We were in Africa. My brain was flooded with euphoria, and all the worries and concerns slipped away. Africa! It was just as I had hoped it would be. For the first time in my life, I could actually feel my ribs expand when I took a breath. Sunlight permeated everything. It soaked through my pores and drenched my skin. Our very first day out on safari, a family of elephants came lumbering down out of the hills and played in the water not fifteen feet away from our jeep. I could feel their monstrous, pounding footfalls deep inside my body. I started to cry, for no reason except that I was so supremely happy. Lisa looked at me, concerned, but I waved her away. "It's just so hopelessly beautiful," I said, and continued to cry throughout the trip. Zebras, gazelle, white rhino, wildebeest: each animal brought new tears.

It was the lions that finally did me in. They were so golden and glorious, it was all too much. Too much beauty. I started to sob and couldn't stop. Our guide looked at Lisa, and she just shook her head. Had I crossed the invisible line that separates me from "normal" people?

I was probably manic, I realized. It added up: None of the other people on safari had started bawling at the sight of two cheetahs humping. Nobody else kept standing up in the jeep and making sweeping pronouncements like "Surely this is how God meant the world to be." And nobody else was spending all night camped outside in a deck chair, staring at the African sky, expecting the stars to speak to them. But recognition of mania is one thing. Doing something about it is something else altogether.

I could double up on some of my medications, I thought. But then, did I really want to miss out on this experience? Who in their right mind would give up the chance to feel Africa so intensely? This was God's country, and I was God's creature. Did I really want a pill to act as a buffer between us?

The danger of mania is always its grandiosity. If nothing else, Africa puts you in your proper place. I felt thoroughly in perspective, a tiny smudge beneath that infinite sky. So no, I concluded, there was no danger of my grandiosity running out of control. But just to be safe, I should probably take my awe and exuberance down a few notches to fit in with the rest of the group. And then I'd let Africa itself act as my antipsychotic: surely it would keep me in better check than any pill ever could.

This worked well enough for the next five days. I toned down my reactions, quieted my pronouncements, and Lisa and the other tourists stopped acting so anxious around me. But marvelous as my experience had been so far, it was all just picture postcard epiphanies. I wanted more. I had come to Africa, like centuries of explorers before me, for answers.

Our guide had promised us a treat for the last day of our safari: we were going to visit a Masai village. "The real thing," he assured us. "Very special, very rare." This village was not usually accessible to tourists, but the guide was related by marriage to one of the tribe and thus was able to get us in. We could smell it long before we arrived: that sharp and savage odor peculiar to the Masai diet of cattle milk and blood. Then a hazy black cloud appeared on the horizon. "The cattle?" I asked the guide. "No. The flies."

I thought he was exaggerating, but when we were within one hundred feet of the village we had to raise our voices to be heard above the angry, buzzing swarm. Flies everywhere. And not your well-mannered American house fly, either. These flies were half the size of my fist. They came at you and stuck to you with a single-minded purpose you had to admire. We were hopelessly outnumbered, but we still slapped and kicked and karate-chopped ourselves until we reached an uneasy truce.

But the flies didn't seem to bother the Masai natives. At first I thought the whole tribe was tattooed; that is, until the tattoos started moving. The villagers simply allowed the flies to crawl all over them, even in and out of their noses and mouths, as if they were a second skin. This might have been picturesque through a viewfinder, but I was far too close to see it for anything but what it really was: a hideous harbinger of disease. Just beneath the crawling black coats were masses of oozing red sores. The little children, in particular, were covered with large, weeping ulcers.

The only other time I had seen skin like this, although on a much lesser scale, was on my last visit with David. Toward the end, the bedsores on his back, buttocks, and thighs had become grossly infected with no hope of healing. But at least they were covered in ointment and sterile gauze bandages, and unpleasant as the sharp ammonia smell permeating his bedside was, it was still an odor my mind could catalogue and place. Whereas this stench had no counterpart in my memory. It smelled of one thing: death.

A wave of nausea flooded me. I could taste the heavy cream and butter the chef had used to scramble my eggs that morning. Breakfast had been delicious. For that matter, dinner the night before had been delicious, too: the tournedos Rossini lightly seared to perfection, the lemon soufflé a marvel of spun sugar and air. In fact, everything about this trip had been delicious—until now. I could feel my mood beginning to plummet.

What right? I asked myself. What possible right have you ever had to be depressed? I thought of my therapist's office, and the thousands of dollars I spent each year, complaining about my life. I thought about the handful of antidepressants I swallowed each morning: one pill alone cost me almost four hundred dollars a month. Add to that the psychopharmacologist I saw every six weeks or so, at three hundred dollars per visit. All totaled, the price of my depression was staggering, more than enough to feed and house and clothe several Masai families for an entire year. What right, what right?

But the question went far deeper than cost. What right did I have to own despair, with such genuine suffering before me? I looked around me at the pockmarked children, and all I could think was, a six-figure lifestyle drove me to suicide.

It's chemical, I told myself. I didn't choose to be manic-depressive. It's as much outside my control as the color of my skin or where I was born. I knew at some primal level that this was logical, and therefore likely to be true. I gradually began to feel a little bit better.

A tug on my shirt made me look down. A little girl, entirely naked but for the beaded hoops in her ears, was standing directly in front of me. Her entire body was covered in sores. Yet she smiled, a smile wide as the savannah, open as the sky. And all the logic in the world made no sense after that. I had no arguments to compete against that smile.

The only question now, and I knew it was the one I had come to Africa to ask, was why? Why in all its many vast permutations: Why did the plague visit this village? Why did my darling David have to die? And why, above all else, was I manic-depressive? Or perhaps the real question was, why did I deserve to be sane?

I fully expected something cataclysmic to happen—a sudden flood, a stampede, a gust of locusts. I waited. Nothing happened. The next morning, the trip over, I left Africa for home.

It was weeks before my dreams finally stopped buzzing. For a while, I truly appreciated my life: I savored every smell, lingered over every sensation, marveled at every creature comfort. Then inevitably, my brain chemistry shifted and my mood plunged back down to despair. Africa, apparently, was not a cure for depression. It only added a new level of guilt to my suffering.

And yes, it was suffering. Despite all my questions to the African sky, when depression finally struck again I not only believed I had the right to suffer, I felt I owned the patent on it. But it would be years before I ever attempted to kill myself again. Each time I thought about suicide, the image of that little Masai girl would flash in my mind. And I still could not argue against that smile.

9

I woke up strapped to a bed, covered in a thick gray charcoal vomit and desperately needing to pee. The only part of me that I could move was my head, and I turned it frantically back and forth, searching for some kind of clue as to where I might be. But no matter how hard I strained against them, the heavy leather restraints pinning me to the bed refused to give way. The edges of the straps were tattered and frayed, and the harder I struggled, the deeper they bit into the tender skin of my wrists and ankles. Good torture points, the inner wrists and ankles.

Had I been in some kind of an accident? A car crash? An earthquake? A fire? Maybe I was severely burned. That would explain the restraints, at least: they didn't want me scratching my skin. I shut my eyes and started to cry. What a horrible thing, to be burned and deformed at such a young age. I sobbed for a while at the top of my lungs, but nobody came. Exhausted, I fell asleep, dreaming of dragon skin.

When I woke, who knows how many hours later (the room had only one overhead light, and no windows), the urge to urinate was so intense I felt sharp shooting pains all around my bladder. I whipped my head back and forth again, but there was no one within the line of my sight. All I noticed this time was the rather peculiar look of the walls. They had a thick, quilted texture to them, almost as if they were . . . padded.

Now what kind of burn victim needs a padded room? I puzzled a while, and then it came to me. Why, one who is out of her mind, of course. And then it all came flooding back: that terrible phone call, just as I was getting ready to leave the house. Strange how the telephone rings just the same, whether it's wonderful news or the end of all life as you know it. I heard the doctor's oddly high-pitched voice: "I'm sorry, Ms. Cheney, but it appears that your father's cancer has metastasized far beyond what we ever expected. It's just a matter of months now. You have my deepest regrets."

I sincerely needed his deepest regrets. I needed everyone's deepest regrets, because I was the one who was going to have to tell my father. The doctor thought it was better that way. Better for him, no doubt. But first, I needed a Valium. Or two. Or three. That's what they were there for, after all—for times when you needed the deepest regrets. I waited for the pills to take effect, but after ten minutes my hands were still shaking too badly to pick up a hairbrush. So I popped a couple more. I'd be damned if I was going to tell my father news like this without my hair properly combed and my makeup perfectly applied. Daddy liked immaculate grooming. He liked me pretty as a peach.

I sat down on the bed and tried to rehearse my speech, but the farthest I got was "Daddy, I'm so sorry," before I burst into tears. Damn the Valium, anyway; it wasn't helping at all. I cursed myself. Why was I relying on the weakest gun in my arsenal? I went to the cupboard and gathered up several fistfuls of bottles and spread them out on the bed: Ativan, Librium, Klonopin, Xanax, and Stelazine. Surely inside one or more of these bottles resided the calm and the courage I needed to face this task.

By nature I'm rather small-boned and petite, but you wouldn't know it from my astounding tolerance to medication. I can take enough pills to knock a Clydesdale off its feet, and at the most I'll just yawn and blink rather drowsily and ask when the next dose is due. So I didn't see any real cause for concern when I shook out a pill from each of these bottles and downed all five at once. Twenty minutes later, I still didn't feel anything, although for the life of me I couldn't seem to get my lipstick to go on straight. It kept wandering up and off my lip line and onto my cheeks. I scrubbed away vigorously at the errant crimson marks, but that only served to smear them further into my already streaky blush.

Bright red cheeks, swollen mouth, and slightly glazed eyes: this was definitely not the look I was going for. I looked like a rather befuddled clown, and my father hated clowns. I started to panic. What if I never managed pretty again? I'd heard of people's hair turning gray overnight from a shock. Maybe it's possible to turn sudden ugly, too. I eyed all the bottles spread out on the bed. Surely another dose or two couldn't hurt. Just to take the edge off this panic. Just to focus my meandering thoughts. Then as soon as I felt a bit more collected, I would drive over to my father's and tell him the news. But not until then. And certainly not yet. I owed him more than collected. I owed him serene.

In search of serenity, I swallowed the next ten pills with a big glass of orange juice, figuring I probably ought to have something in my stomach to help them dissolve. I couldn't remember the last time I'd eaten—this morning? yesterday? the day before? Who cared? Food was just one more item that used to matter that meant nothing to me anymore. Food, sex, books, movies—all those reliable little pleasures of life before the cancer seemed somehow absurd and trivial now. Watching my father's eyes flutter and close when the morphine finally kicked in: now *that* was joy. A ninety-eight point six thermometer reading: that was ecstasy.

I knew that a prolonged lack of appetite is usually a good indicator that I'm manic, but that was certainly not the case at the moment. My current mood on a scale of one to ten was a minus five. But who wouldn't be depressed under these circumstances? Sure, I was secretly suicidal. I longed for death, I daydreamed about it, it was all I thought about in my spare time. But I had no intention of acting on my fantasies—not yet, not while Daddy was still alive. He needed me. I loved him. It was as simple as that.

So when I tossed back the next big handful of pills, there was nothing suicidal about the gesture. I'd simply forgotten about the last dose. I was finally starting to feel twinges of serenity—a warmth in my toes, a pleasant humming in my ears—and I just wanted to speed the process along. But when I went to put the orange juice away, the ceiling and floor suddenly tilted at odd angles, and the next thing I knew I was flat on the linoleum. The cold, smooth tile felt good against my flushed cheeks. It dawned on me as I lay there that I was actually happy, happier than I had been in months. I knew that there was something I was supposed to be doing, something important I was supposed to remember, but for the life of me I couldn't think what that thing was. All that really mattered was the here and now: the cool kiss of the linoleum, the soothing song of the refrigerator. I closed my eyes and was about to drift into sleep when the telephone rang, jolting me awake.

The phone didn't ring very much anymore, except when it was news from the doctors. As Daddy grew sicker and I became more depressed, I pulled away from the world I'd known. My friends meant well, but their expressions of sympathy only made me feel more alone. They were never quite the right words somehow, and they were never anywhere near enough. The truth was, the battle lines had already been drawn. It was my father and me against the world. There was no room for anyone else.

The phone kept ringing, and I tried to get up, but the bones in my legs had melted to mush and wouldn't support my weight. So I crawled on my hands and knees across the kitchen floor, and into the bedroom. I noticed when I went to reach for the phone that my hand was still shaking rather violently.

"Hello?" I mumbled. I couldn't quite decipher the words, but I recognized the voice immediately. It was my ex-boyfriend Jeff, making one of his ubiquitous bicoastal checkup calls. Ever since my father had been diagnosed several months before, Jeff had taken to calling me at odd hours just to make sure that I was still alive and able to answer the phone. It was kind, and I sincerely appreciated the gesture, but I didn't feel like talking just then. I felt like crawling back to the kitchen floor and listening to the refrigerator sing its sweet hymn. I explained just that as clearly as I could into the receiver. Jeff later told me it came out sounding like one long sodden slur of vowels, without a single consonant.

"Have you taken any medication tonight?" he asked me, and for some reason I found that question so hilarious I burst out laughing and couldn't stop. I laughed so hard that tears coursed down my face. When I raised my hand to wipe them away, I suddenly remembered other tears, from times that were not so funny. I began to cry in earnest. "No!" I shouted. "I don't remember, and you can't make me!" Then I slammed down the phone as emphatically as I could, so hard I actually cracked the receiver. That struck me as funny for some reason, too, and all at once I was laughing again, laughing until I sobbed—but careful this time not to touch the tears.

And that, apparently, is how the paramedics got called. All I can remember after that is taking another large handful of pills, a double handful this time, because I was finally starting to feel the effects and the effects felt pretty damned good. Then I crawled back to the refrigerator, caressed the cold tile, and knew nothing more, until I woke up staring with incomprehension at padded green walls.

A door that was hidden beneath that padding suddenly opened, and a large troupe of white-coated persons walked in. I estimated fifteen or so at one glance, twelve men and three women. Some of the younger white coats held a bit back, so I assumed that they must be mere students or residents. An elderly gentleman with a short grizzled beard stepped up to my bed with a file and a pen and began barking questions. Did I know my name? Did I know where I was? Did I know who the vice president of the United States was? At this point I stopped him and explained apologetically that I really, truly needed to pee. I would be happy to give him all the info he wanted, including the names of all the cabinet members that I could recall, if he would just let me visit the ladies' room first.

He sucked on his pen and studied the file. "No, we can't undo your restraints just yet," he said. "We have you down as actively suicidal."

"You think this was a suicide attempt?" I laughed. "Believe me, if I was going to try to commit suicide, I'd take a lot more than just a few handfuls of pills. I'd take whole bottles, dozens of them, and I'd wash it all down with quarts and quarts of tequila. I have nowhere near enough pills saved up yet to do it right. And I still haven't figured out how to make a proper noose, or found the right kind of plastic bag to tie over my head. . . ."

My voice trailed off, as I noticed that several of the younger white coats were scribbling furiously in their little notebooks. The rest of them were just staring at me openmouthed with fascination, as if I were a real live lab rat suddenly granted the gift of speech. I sensed that I was making a losing argument. Certainly my words had not had the desired effect on old Dr. Graybeard. He simply turned and addressed his entourage: "Note the attempt to persuade by hyperbole," he said. "This is characteristic of the grandiosity we can expect in acute mania."

I wasn't manic, but what did it matter? "Doctor," I said. "I'm perfectly willing to be manic, or hypomanic, or cyclothymic, or whatever it takes to get these restraints off. But first, could you please just call a nurse to accompany me to the bathroom?"

He cocked his head and stared at me. "Are you willing to admit to attempting suicide?"

I took a deep breath, then exhaled slowly. "No, I'm sorry," I said. "But it's simply not true. I'll admit to making an error of judgment, but I wasn't trying to kill myself. You have to understand: it's a point of honor with me right now. I can't kill myself because my father needs me. You see, he's . . ."

"Then I have no other option but to order a fourteen-day hold," he said. "You'll have to stay here on the locked ward for now. Maybe in a few days, if we see any improvement, you can be transferred over to the inpatient unit. We'll have to wait and see."

He dashed off a few quick notes on the chart and handed it to the young man standing next to him. "Make sure she gets the Haldol right away," he said. "And Thorazine PRN." He turned around and walked out the door, the white coats scrambling in his wake.

I stared at the place where the door had once been. It was now a seamless expanse of quilted green. Then I heard it: an ominous series of click-click-clicks, the unmistakable chorus of lock and key. Instinctively, I started thrashing from side to side. I wriggled, I squirmed, I tried to wrench myself free, but to no avail. The air was growing increasingly thin, and I couldn't catch a decent breath. No doubt I was on the verge of a full-blown panic attack, but ironically, my bursting bladder came to my rescue. I couldn't think about anything else—except, perversely, running streams and gushing fountains and mighty, thunderous waterfalls.

Just give up and go, my body demanded. But one tiny sliver of my spirit resisted, and I knew it was right. There was more at stake here than just wetting my bed. The greatest challenge of being mentally ill is always, despite the enormous odds stacked up against you, to maintain some sense of dignity. But my body didn't give a damn: it just wanted to pee. I tried shouting as loudly as I could, a range of exhortations from "Nurse!" to "Orderly!" to plain old "Help!," but no one came. I seriously contemplated shouting "Fire!," but the lawyer in me wouldn't cross that line.

I leaned back against the pillow and sighed. "It's just your body," I gently reassured myself. "They haven't touched your mind. They don't possess your soul. You're still intact—you'll just be a little bit wetter is all."

I took a deep breath, then let my muscles go. The urine erupted in rhythmic spurts, strong pulsing contractions that gradually eased to a warm steady stream, then to a seemingly endless trickle, before it finally slowed and stopped altogether.

I looked down, amazed. Who knew that my body could hold so much liquid? I was soaked all the way from my waist to my toes, and the sheet was not just wet, it was sopping. Released of its burden, my body felt like it was floating. My mind hovered somewhere up near the ceiling, curiously detached from the sodden spectacle that was strapped beneath the sheet. I fell asleep to the tune of urine tinkling from the bed to the floor.

I woke to a light glaring straight in my eyes. "Wake up!" scolded a voice somewhere behind the light. "Just look what you did. Now was that nice?" A blurry outline of a heavyset woman came into my view. She was gesturing with a penlight to the dripping sheet. "Not nice, but necessary," I said. "I tried to—"

"I tried to, I tried to," she mocked me in a high, snappy voice. "That's what they all say. Well, we'll just have to try a little harder next time, won't we?" Then she whipped the sheet off the bed in one swift, deft motion. The tail end of it slapped me right in the face and I started to cry out, but I caught myself in time. Not now, not with her. I rearranged my features to look as penitent as I could. "I'm sorry to have caused you so much trouble," I said. "But do you have any idea when they'll be taking off these restraints?"

"That's not my job," the nurse replied. "I'm just supposed to give you the meds—and clean up the mess," she added, with a look of disgust. The next thing I knew, she'd jabbed a needle in my arm.

"But wait," I said, as a warm, woozy feeling began to flood through my veins. "I'm sure there's been some kind of horrid mistake. I never meant to kill my—" But before I could even finish the word, I had drifted off into a strange, heavy sleep that felt remarkably like drowning.

When next I woke, it was to Dr. Graybeard poking my shoulder with his pen. I looked around him: yes, the white coats were all assembled, too. "So, now are you willing to admit that you tried to kill yourself?" he asked me.

I glanced down and noticed that while the sheet had been changed, I was still lying on the same urine-soaked mattress. That decided me.

"All right, Doctor, I admit it. I *was* trying to kill myself," I said. "Now can I get out of these straps?"

I could swear a fleeting smile crossed the doctor's face. He pulled a large set of keys from his pocket, fiddled with them for a moment, then matched one to my cuffs. I have never heard a more melodious sound than the four successive clicks that heralded my release. I clapped my hands in sheer delight, then wriggled my legs up in the air. To hell with dignity, just for the moment: I was free! A couple of the white coats way in the back started to giggle. Dr. Graybeard effectively silenced them with a single frown.

"Now, young lady, since you've cooperated, your treatment can finally begin," he said. "We're going to transfer you to the inpatient unit. You'll meet others there with problems just like your own. I'm sure you will enjoy that."

Trying hard not to let my eyes betray me, I smiled at him and asked, "If I do well on the inpatient unit, can we renegotiate the fourteen-day hold?"

He didn't smile back, but then he didn't frown, either. "We'll see" is all he said, then he stuffed his pen inside his shirt pocket and walked away, his entourage close on his heels.

"We'll see." "We'll see." What the hell did that mean? With my mother, it always used to mean no; with my father, it always meant yes. I couldn't decide which parental figure the doctor more closely resembled. Nor did it matter, I supposed. The point was, I was the child. I curled up into a tight little ball and sucked gently on the sore, inflamed skin of my inner wrist.

The inpatient unit felt just like elementary school, with plenty of rules and regularly scheduled activities. There were brightly colored beads to string, and pots to paint, and decoupage, and jigsaw puzzles—lots and lots of jigsaw puzzles. Sandwiched somewhere in between the fun and games was "group." That's what we called it, "group." I wouldn't call it therapy, because not much of a healing nature took place in those cramped and airless rooms. Somebody sobbed. Somebody else went on about his mother. Nobody talked about the here-and-now, the unbearable truth of where we were and what we thought about each other. Mostly we struggled against the stupor, stifling overmedicated yawns and twitching and fidgeting in our chairs like restless six-year-olds.

Of all the rules they handed to me when I checked in—there were dozens of mimeographed pages—they forgot to tell me the most important one: never stare at a paranoid schizophrenic. I discovered this my very first day on the unit, when I made the mistake of staring at Chuck, a big, burly young man with silver-blond hair and the whitest skin I had ever seen. Extremely pale people are always inherently interesting to me, since as a redhead I've spent my whole life defending my pallor.

We were sitting in the cafeteria, at opposite ends of a long metal table, when Chuck's enormous arm suddenly reached all the way down past the other diners, past the trays and cups and assorted utensils. He grabbed my Styrofoam cup of Coke and crushed it slowly in his fist. Brown liquid spouted everywhere, landing not just on me but on several of the other people sitting at the table. No one said a word except Chuck, who stared unblinking at me as his fingers choked the life out of my Coca-Cola.

"What do you think you're looking at?" he growled.

"Absolutely nothing," I quickly replied.

"If I ever catch you looking again . . ." His fingers finished the sentence for him, as they dropped the mangled remains of my cup onto the table.

I instantly averted my eyes, but it was hard to know where to look, since four of the other six patients were schizophrenics, too. Fortunately, there were also two obsessive-compulsives, who didn't seem to mind if my glance rested casually on them in passing. But the truth was, I didn't much like looking at them. One was a cutter, or rather an eraser, to be exact. He had rubbed off every exposed inch of skin and was frantically picking and gnawing at the sores. The other was a young woman who might have been pretty were it not for the bald patches dotting her scalp and her utter lack of any eyelashes or brows. That didn't keep her from plucking, though. Pluck,

pluck, pluck, pluck, all day long, with an almost orgasmic moan of satisfaction each time she managed to pull out a hair.

I knew the clinical term for this, of course: trichotillomania. But a fat lot of good my fancy education was doing me now. There was no one to impress. I was as isolated in here as I was in the outside world. I didn't dare say much to the clinicians assigned to my case for fear I'd never see daylight again. And I didn't dare talk to the patients, either, because they didn't feel like real people to me. They felt like walking diagnoses, and quite frankly, they terrified me. I didn't belong here, and I certainly wasn't one of them—not yet, and I wanted to keep it that way.

I didn't have any visitors, by choice. When I was finally allowed access to a phone a few days into my stay on the unit, I only called two people: my father and Jeff. Daddy, of course, was too sick to come and too doped-up to understand what had happened. I finally told him I was on vacation, a concept he still understood. I debated calling a few other people, but to be honest, I was too ashamed to let them see me like this, doing the Thorazine shuffle in frowsy old hospital slippers. Better to wait until I was back home and could turn it all into a story.

There was certainly no lack of material. The latest arrival on the unit was a bearded young man in his early thirties, with piercing blue eyes. I was hoping for another manic-depressive, but as soon as he opened his mouth, I knew I was in for a different diagnosis entirely.

"Hello," he said. "I'm Jesus Christ. You can call me Jesus. Or Lord, if you like."

"Lord what?" I asked, lamely trying to be funny. I mean, it

had to be a joke, right? Jesus Christ in a mental asylum. What a cliché.

"Why, Lord God, of course," he said, with a puzzled frown. "Or perhaps you are Jewish? If so, it's okay if you just call me Christ."

"No, I'm born and bred Catholic all right," I told him.

"Then you should have genuflected when you walked in," he admonished me. He quickly made the sign of the cross in the air. "I forgive you this time," he said. "But don't let it happen again." Then he looked at me with those laser beam eyes, and a sudden chill seized hold of my heart. What if Jesus was indeed alive today—was this where he'd end up? There's a very fine line, indistinguishable at times, between charismatic and crazy.

But our Jesus seemed to be harmless enough, unless you forgot to genuflect when you approached him, in which case he would burst out screaming—eerie, high-pitched, rhythmic shrieks—and he wouldn't stop until the offending party knelt, or a nurse administered a sedative, whichever came first. But once appeased, his eyes returned to their old limpid blue, his face relaxed into a beatific smile, and he proceeded to walk around the room bestowing blessings on everything in his path: the patients, the armchairs, the coffee urn, the jigsaw puzzles.

A word about those puzzles. There were at least a dozen of them stacked up on the tables, waiting to be assembled, and a dozen or so more spread out on the floor in varying degrees of completion. We were strongly encouraged, even urged, to work at them. Jigsaw puzzles, I later learned, were not really jigsaw puzzles at all. They were "occupational therapy," and

I was billed three hundred dollars an hour for the privilege of playing with them.

But the truth was, I was so bored out of my mind, I was grateful for anything that kept me even minimally occupied. So I took to the puzzles with a vengeance. I didn't care what the final picture was supposed to be: English farmhouse, Egyptian pharaoh, Mt. McKinley, Van Gogh's *Starry Night*, sunrise over Montebello, sunset over Malibu. It didn't matter, I worked them all. Or at least I tried to. But without exception, a handful of pieces was always missing from each puzzle. If you weren't already crazy by the time you started, you were certain to be so by the time you finished—or rather, failed to finish. For an ardent perfectionist like me, it was absolute torture. For the obsessive-compulsives, who couldn't stop trying to make the same wrong piece fit over and over and over again, it bordered on cruel.

Little things like a missing puzzle piece matter when you're no longer in control of your environment, when every decision is made for you, from what you eat to what you wear to when you sleep to whom you are allowed to associate with. I found myself jealously guarding my work in progress. It was my own little sphere of autonomy, however flawed and unfinished. In fact, despite all my efforts to be the perfect mental patient, I nearly lost my composure one day when I walked into the puzzle room and discovered one of the schizophrenics eating an ice cap off my Mt. McKinley. "What the hell do you think you're doing?" I demanded, forgetting that one should never confront a schizophrenic directly. It activates all his well-oiled alarms. "I was thirsty," he said, and I was so charmed by the

Alice in Wonderland logic of that, I smiled and broke him off another big piece.

Smiles were hard to come by on the ward. I had been there seven days already, and I could count my smiles on the fingers of one hand—my genuine smiles, that is. I was nothing but smiles when I dealt with the doctors. I figured the only way to escape the fourteen-day hold was to claim a sudden epiphany, so when I met with them I was all aglow with my newly discovered appreciation of life. Since I rarely saw the same doctor twice in a row, it was hard to tell what kind of overall impression I was making. But I did overhear them once talking about me out in the hall. "Excellent insight," one of them said. "Strong motivation." "Self-imposed integration."

I wasn't quite sure what that last phrase meant, but I figured any kind of integration was probably good. So why in the name of all that was fair and just was I still on a fourteen-day hold? Seven more days. It was impossible to imagine seven more days of beaded leather moccasins; of menacing albinos and screaming messiahs; of interminable empty daylight hours and drugged-to-oblivion nights. I should be with my father now, I thought, and a desperate ache shot through me. Seven more days, and I was sure my sanity would explode all over these walls, mingling nicely with the bilious green wallpaper.

For the first time since I'd landed in the hospital, I craved the suffocating black nothingness that followed my nightly shot. I couldn't bear the pretense anymore of planning, manipulating, scheming to get free, when the truth was, I was trapped on a psycho ward and there wasn't a damned thing I could do about it. It didn't matter that I'd successfully litigated countless civil rights cases over the years, including one that had gone all the way up to the United States Supreme Court. This wasn't a courtroom. This wasn't even real life. This was Kafka-land, where all the puzzles have pieces missing.

I woke up early the next morning, decidedly depressed. I hoped I didn't have any doctors' interviews that day. It was going to be hard enough just to maintain my civility with the rest of the patients, let alone try to sparkle with newfound drive and resolution while a thick-witted white coat took notes. I glanced in the mirror, stuck my tongue out at my reflection, and halfheartedly dragged a comb through my hair. Then I shuffled down the hall to join the rest of the patients at breakfast.

There were only two others in the dining room at that time: Jesus Christ and Chuck. I studiously averted my eyes from Chuck while dropping a quick half-curtsy in Christ's direction, which I hoped would suffice for a genuflection at that early hour. It apparently did, because Jesus Christ scooted down and invited me to join them. I would have preferred to eat alone, but I didn't want to be rude—or more important, perceived as rude, especially by Chuck. I grabbed a box of milk and a carton of Cheerios, and sat down at their table.

Chuck and Jesus were having quite an animated discussion about, of all things, the Virgin Mary. Chuck swore she was a brunette; Jesus insisted she was a blonde. I decided to throw my two cents in: "Well, I happen to know for a fact that Mary Magdalene was a redhead," I said, sprinkling sugar on my cereal.

"You shouldn't have said that," Chuck immediately reproached me. "Now we're in for it."

"What do you mean?" I started to ask, but then it was all too apparent what Chuck had meant. Jesus had reached a hand into his sweats and was enthusiastically fondling himself in plain sight.

"He does that every time you mention her," Chuck said.

"Who?" I asked. "Mary Magdalene?"

Jesus groaned and redoubled his efforts. I was embarrassed and amused and frightened, all at the same time. I sought support from the only other person in the room: my eyes pleaded with Chuck's for some sense of protection. He was, after all, almost a foot taller and fifty pounds heavier than Jesus Christ. A big guy, with an even bigger disease. The instant our eyes met, he stood up, jolting the table so hard that all the milk sloshed out of my cereal and his orange juice carton went spinning onto the floor. Then he snatched up his plastic fork, scrambled eggs still clinging to it, and before I realized what was happening he had crossed over to my side of the table, grabbed me from behind, and thrust the tines of the fork up against my neck.

"What do you think you're looking at?" he snarled in my ear. I didn't know what to answer. I was afraid to move even the slightest bit, for fear he would puncture my throat with the fork. I fervently wished I'd paid more attention to basic anatomy in high school. I wasn't quite sure where my jugular was, but I was pretty sure Chuck had it covered. So I simply held myself quiet and still, as still as I could, given the violent trembling that had suddenly overtaken my limbs.

Jesus had finished his self-ministrations by then, and his eyes had returned to their former sky-blue serenity. He smiled mildly at Chuck and stroked him on the forearm. I could feel Chuck's grip around my windpipe begin to loosen, imperceptibly at first, and then all at once he dropped his arm to his side. The fork clattered to the ground, and I quickly kicked it under the table. Then my knees gave way beneath me, and I found myself staring up at the ceiling; and then, I have no idea how many minutes later, into the eyes of Jesus Christ.

"What's your real name?" I asked him. "I mean, what name did your mother give you?"

"Henry," he said.

"Henry, you just saved my life. How can I ever repay you?"

He helped me to my feet. We were still the only ones in the cafeteria at that early hour, except for the wait staff, which was busy rubberizing eggs and solidifying oatmeal. Even so, Henry whispered.

"I want you to forgive him."

"Are you kidding?" I said. "This is my ticket out." Even as I was laying there on the floor, I was thinking how I could turn this incident to my advantage. It didn't matter that my arms and legs were still trembling, or that a scream was tickling the back of my throat. A lawyer's brain is always working— evaluating, calculating, debating the odds. The face of my first-year torts professor inexplicably popped in my head, and above it two words glared in bright neon: "foreseeable risk." I knew that the hospital clearly had notice of Chuck's dangerous quirks, because the day he'd first confronted me in the cafeteria, I'd made a point of mentioning it to the head nurse. "Oh, he's like that with everyone" was her reply. At the time, I'd thought it a singularly inadequate response. Now it filled me with lawyerly glee.

"Seriously, Henry," I said. "I'm out of here. They've got exposure, they'll have to let me go."

"If you report this, they'll take him back to the locked ward and he'll never get out."

A visceral memory came back to me of that horrible room with padded walls and no windows. The narrow bed with the leather restraints. The tune of the yellow tinkles. Empathy began to invade my heart.

"He's just like you," Henry said. "He's sick."

Just like me? Just like me? He was nothing like me. He lived at the beck and call of a monster that made him do terrible, dangerous things. Whereas I—I sat down hard on the metal bench and watched Chuck heap mounds of sugar into his tea. Oh hell, who was I kidding? The truth was, he was exactly like me. I had a monster living inside me, too. Who else had commanded me to keep taking pills, handful after handful, just to kill the noise inside my head, when my father needed me alive and sane?

I realized then why I was avoiding all the other patients. They were all potential mirrors. What I really feared wasn't the insanity of strangers. What I feared the most was my own disease. I was terrified I would catch a glimpse of myself in passing.

A few people began coming into the cafeteria then, accompanied by an attendant. The time was now or never.

"Chuck," I said, dropping my eyes. "Please pass the sugar."
Henry beamed at me, and oddly enough, I felt good.

I'd like to say that after that, we all became fast friends.
But Chuck was carted off somewhere that very afternoon—
shock therapy, was the word on the unit. Henry and I did
become allies of a sort. He was good company, when his
meds were working. We became mealtime buddies, along
with several other patients whose symptoms were somewhat
less frightening than Chuck's: Theresa, a near-catatonic
depressive; Jim, a manic-depressive who couldn't stop talking,
his every third word an obscenity; and Allison, who saw
visions and auras and frankly didn't seem that much crazier
to me than the average psychic on Venice Beach. We shared
the instant intimacy of the oppressed, finding endless topics
of discussion in the apathy of the nurses, the incompetence
of the doctors, the shocking injustice of the health care
system. Mostly, however, we talked about what it was like to
be mentally ill—the same subject we assiduously avoided in
group.

"You seem better," Henry said to me one afternoon, after
I'd laughed so hard at one of Jim's riffs of profanity that I'd spit
up my tea.

I almost didn't want to admit it, I'd become so safe and
familiar with despair, but it was true. I felt better. And it
apparently showed, because that afternoon, just a few days shy
of my fourteen-day hold, I was told I was being released.

It was awkward saying good-bye to the other patients. I felt
intensely guilty about leaving them, as if I was the only one
walking away whole from a train wreck. So to assuage my guilt,

I decided to stage a rebellion my last night there. I knew it was probably too little too late, but at least it was a start.

I assembled all five of the remaining patients and led them into the so-called occupational therapy room. There we pounced on the puzzles: we decapitated Mt. McKinley, we eviscerated Van Gogh's *Starry Night*. We shuffled up all the sunrises and sunsets until they were no longer distinguishable from one another. Then we threw all the pieces together into one big pile on the floor, and we war-danced around it. We stamped, we stomped, we whooped and wahooed until the head nurse came running into the room and ordered us all to our beds. But by then the damage was done. No one would ever be able to make another mouthless Mona Lisa again. The age of one-eyed pharaohs and legless ballerinas was definitely over.

I left the hospital the next morning, and was never so happy as when the taxicab finally dropped me off at my own little gate. My house struck me as singularly beautiful somehow, for all its advanced state of disrepair. I walked through every one of the rooms, admiring the smooth white walls. I had never fully appreciated their purity before. For the rest of my life, I vowed to myself, I would never have anything else in my homes but plain white walls.

I sat down at my desk and stared at the phone. My answering machine flashed "Full." I knew I had a great many calls, a great many explanations to make, but my first order of business had to be my father. As I picked up the phone to dial his number, I couldn't help but think back to that very first Valium that had set this whole chain of events in motion.

How terrified I'd been that afternoon, so frightened that all I'd wanted was oblivion. Well, I'd had my fair share of oblivion, and I had no desire for a Valium now. In fact, my body rebelled at the thought of any drug entering my system. I no longer wanted to fuzz the sharp edges with medication. I liked them sharp.

I dialed the telephone and let it ring—once, twice, and then a familiar Kansas twang answered. "Hello?" said the voice I loved dearest in all the world.

"It's me," I said. "I'm back."

IO

I met the doctor of my dreams at my father's deathbed. I wasn't exactly looking my best, but Alex didn't seem to mind. Two weeks later I was back in the ER, this time on my own. Grief burns like hell, but it doesn't cause a 104-degree fever. I knew what that thick yellow sticky stuff coming up from my lungs meant. I didn't care.

Alex's hand was on my forehead when I woke up. His eyes were brilliant, like emeralds lit from behind. I love green eyes. And black hair. And well-worn scrubs. Then he smiled, and they tell me I fainted.

He came to see me several times after I was admitted, although technically I wasn't on his turf. He brought me books—we both had a thing for F. Scott Fitzgerald—and read me passages out loud. What can you do when you've just lost your father and a green-eyed doctor leans over your hospital bed and recites, "So we beat on, boats against the current, borne back ceaselessly into the past. . . ."

I was charmed, but reluctant to respond. Dad's death had drained me of all the softer emotions, plus I was still smarting from my recent breakup with Rick. (Despite all my agonizing over the ethics of our illicit affair, he had finally been the one to call it quits.) So I didn't allow Alex to get too close, but apparently it was close enough. He kept on coming to see me, even after I was released from the hospital.

Pursue and retreat; pursue and retreat. This quickly became the rhythm of our relationship. He'd call, I wouldn't answer. He'd ask, I'd say no. Then one day, out of nowhere, I'd call him back. I'd say yes, of course I want to get together, what took you so long to ask?

Valentine's Day. The reservation had been almost impossible to get, and the pressure on me to show up at a scheduled time was almost more than I could bear. But who knows what stars had aligned in my favor that night? I was all aglow—skin, eyes, hair, it all worked, even that less-than-little black dress that made me shiver with immodesty.

There were candles at our table. The waiters were gracious, the sommelier was impressed by Alex's choice, and the Chilean sea bass was perfect. Our conversation seemed lighter than usual, drifting from subject to subject, barely touching down before it floated away again. And then he stopped talking altogether, leaned over and took my hand. My God, I thought, he's going to propose. "You're so perfect," he said. "What's *wrong* with you?"

I could have told Alex that I was manic-depressive. He's a doctor, he might have understood. But I chose, rightly or wrongly, to say nothing, just smile, and say nothing still, until he finally looked down at his menu. When he raised his head, he said, "I'm getting tired. Do we really want to stay for dessert?"

He probably wouldn't have believed me, anyway. A real illness has symptoms that show up on tests, is evidenced on the flesh. But I'd kept the real ups and downs out of Alex's sight, hidden behind unanswered phones and declined invitations. I was "perfect" when he saw me because I was perfectly hypomanic: three-quarters of the way to mania, at that point where all things, but mostly the person you are with, seem utterly fascinating. I don't need candlelight then because I am naturally incandescent. If I smiled at you, you caught the glow. If I touched you, you felt the fire. You never realized how cold you had been until we kissed.

Maybe if I had said "manic depression" just right—with my eyes and not my lips—he would have sighed with relief and told me all the ways that we could treat it. But it's one thing to be clinically compassionate. It's something else altogether when that perfect girl of yours sits across from you at dinner, and she's somebody you've never met.

We did end up staying for dessert that last night—raspberry something with white chocolate mousse. It was delicious but mine tasted vaguely of tears. I excused myself and went up to the ladies' room. I stared at the mirror. He wanted imperfect?

I'd show him just how imperfect perfection can be. I'd start
returning his phone calls when I was manic. I'd talk and
talk, I wouldn't let him get off, wouldn't care if he had an
emergency. Or maybe I'd ask him over in the midst of a really
bad depression. . . .

No. Not even in my wildest revenge fantasies could I
imagine him seeing me then. Nobody sees me then. My
doctors never do, and no one ever will, because I turn into
something so foul and loathsome that even I have to drape
towels over the mirrors until the worst of it passes. I don't have
the will then, or the desire or the energy to force myself out
of bed long enough to bathe. My hair turns lank and oily, the
sheets grow stale, and tiny demons ooze from all my pores. My
mouth is the only muscle in my body that will move, and even
then I sometimes have to force it open and closed with my
hands. But still I eat, and eat, whatever's in the house. Sugar
straight out of the box. Pasta, cooked or uncooked, who cares?
Furry cheese. I eat until I fall asleep, and then I wake and eat
whatever is left on my pillow. Ten pounds of depression, and
that less-than-little black dress barely fits one of my thighs. This
is hardly narcissism: it's a genuine crisis, if you're dating a man
who's only ever seen you in a perfect size six.

That perfect size six stared back at me from the ladies'
room mirror. What would be so unforgivably awful, I asked it,
if I were to muss up my hair and rub off my mascara, and go
rejoin Alex with this little raspberry seed still stuck between my
front teeth? What if I didn't reapply my fading lipstick tonight,
tomorrow, or the next time I saw him? Or what if I snapped

one of the buttons off the back of my dress? Normal people go out missing buttons, I see it all the time.

I knew the answer. I can't do it because I simply can't afford to look disheveled in public. A hundred years ago, insanity was diagnosed by appearance—the so-called science of physiognomy. We haven't come all that far since then. I know the snake pit is still alive and writhing because I've been there, except now it's called County General. I was in County for two weeks once following a suicide attempt, and not a single patient strapped down in the locked ward beside me was well-groomed, even clean. But then neither was I, after lying in my own urine for hours, unable to kick free of the sheets. Insanity looks bad and smells even worse.

So when you have a tendency to go mad every so often, it isn't safe to be unkempt, ever—not in your manner, your speech, and especially not in your looks. Sometimes I think that a hundred-dollar haircut is all that stands between me and a fourteen-day hold.

Still, I felt like I owed Alex something. He had given me back the illusion of normalcy, the idea that life actually revolved around decisions like: does the blue sweater go better with my eyes than the green, and what shoes should I wear with this dress? And so it was my thank-you present to him to always show up pretty and well-dressed and happy to be alive. It was the most I could give: the appearance of sanity.

Needless to say, I left the ladies' room that evening with smooth hair, perfect teeth, fresh red lips—and all my buttons intact.

II

I hadn't planned on being manic. For months,
I'd looked forward to the writing workshop I was scheduled to
attend at the Esalen Institute in Big Sur, California. David's
death had convinced me that it was finally time to get serious
about my writing. But first, I'd get a long, deep massage, soak
in the hot tubs, slow down, and rejuvenate. Work had been
particularly hectic of late, what with back-to-back trials and
screaming studio bosses and a cocaine-addled client who
couldn't keep his hands off the phone.

Esalen was the perfect place to find my breath again.
Picture twenty-seven acres of wild wood, green lawns, and
gardens, bounded by cliffs that drop off into the sea.

A carefully cultivated quiet nourishes thought, a silence disturbed only by the boom and crash of the ocean.

Silence: my least favorite sound when I'm manic. I wanted to talk, I needed to talk, words pressed up so hard against the roof of my mouth I felt like I had to spit to breathe. One doesn't spit in Paradise; and it doesn't make a very good impression on the first day of a workshop. I desperately wanted to connect with these people and belong to this place, to pass as a writer among writers. So I managed, by clamping my jaw shut and sucking on my tongue, to get through most of the introductory small talk with responsive nods and a tight-lipped smile. By the time we finally turned to writing, my pen was frantic with all the things I'd left unsaid.

I made it through the night. I even made it through the next morning and three-quarters of the afternoon, at which point I excused myself after a violent fit of coughing. By then the words were backed up so deep in my throat that even tongue-sucking couldn't keep them down. I ran to the edge of the cliffs, where the boom and crash were loudest, and howled. I howled like a moon-sick dog until the sky finally turned black and every light in every window was extinguished. Then I crept back into my bungalow and pretended to sleep.

My body rebelled the second my head hit the pillow. Colors kept exploding behind my closed eyes. Words and numbers glowed and pulsed like neon signs, unintelligible but urgent. I hadn't slept in five days. I had forgotten how.

I fled at the first pale glimmer of light. In my rush, I had left my leather jacket behind. Although my new peach sweater was lovely, it was merely a light silk blend. My socks were simply cotton. Within ten minutes I had lost all sensation in my toes and earlobes, and the tips of my fingers were alarmingly white. But I couldn't go back to the bungalow. Someone was bound to see me. There was nothing left to do but jog in circles, fast as I could, round and round the beautifully manicured gardens with their neatly tended rock borders, tight little fussy lines of rock that squeezed my feet like tiny stone pincers. The last thing I needed was a bordered edge telling me where I shouldn't go.

I had to keep moving. Carmel was only an hour or so up the coast, and class didn't start until much, much later. There was still time—for what, I didn't know. For more.

The ride up the coast was eventful only because of the increasingly heavy rain and the red light flashing on my dashboard. The brake, it said. What about it? Was it on? No. I slammed my open palm against the glass. Not a flicker. If the brake wasn't on, and the light wouldn't go off, then I'd let the guys at Zipper Porsche back in L.A. figure it out. It was the wrong car, anyway, too big and muscular for me. Girls should own Carreras, not 928s, but at least it was a good car to be driving on a day like this: a road warrior against the wet, winding asphalt, where every curve drops off into a rain-shrouded abyss.

The damned brake light stayed on all the way to Carmel. There was a funny smell coming up through the floorboard, too, like charcoal smoldering on a rubber grill. I pulled over at the first sight of town, cursing the stupid car and the stinging rain, and opened up the hood. Smoke and fumes everywhere, overcoming the rain. Maybe the light had meant something after all.

There weren't any Porsche guys in Carmel, just a 76 Station that didn't have time. I hadn't reached the obnoxious stage yet; I was just on the edge, but it didn't show. I simply expected you to do what I wanted you to do, because of course that's what you wanted to do all along. You just didn't know it yet. Very, very charming, with a lawyer's bite and a couple of twenty-dollar bills to back up my smile.

They could fix it, they said, whatever it was, in about two hours. That was fine, it would give me just enough time to do a little shopping before I headed back. I would buy something for every person in my class. I didn't really know them all yet, but it didn't really matter. Something bright, something absurd, something to make the sky blue again. . . . And there it was, right across the street, a quaint hand-lettered sign on a small timbered storefront: High as a Kite. Perfect, perfect! They had every style of kite imaginable—Japanese kites shaped like huge paper lanterns, orange carp kites dangling long string tails, fighter kites that swooped and killed like falcons—all so colorful, so silly, so just what I wanted! I bought a dozen plus two more for luck, because you never know when a kite might come in handy.

Fitting fourteen kites inside my car was a bit tricky, but the service station guys gave me a hand. They had fixed the problem and sent me off with a warning about the storm coming due. Coming due didn't mean here yet, and the brake light wasn't on anymore. None of the lights that shouldn't be were on. There was still time for more.

I think I was the only person on the road back to Esalen. It was quiet. Too quiet.

Serious cars have serious sound systems. I had the biggest bully of them all: a Blaupunkt. You could stick the Partridge Family in that sucker and it would come out sounding like heavy metal. And due to a postkite purchase, I had the perfect tape for the moment: Melissa Etheridge's latest about love and despair and always wanting the wrong woman. Trapped in a storm, surrounded by fury, what could better match my mood? I pulled over to a rest stop, cranked the sound up, and let Melissa rage against the wind: "If I wanted to, I could do anything right / I could dance with the devil on a Saturday night . . ."

Almost perfect, but not enough. I lowered all the windows and let the rain lash my face. The wind whipped through the interior, rattling the kites I had stacked on the front seat and under the deck lid. I reached back to tie them down, and it struck me: what better time to fly a kite than in a storm? Why should anything ever be tethered? I unwound the fighter kite's string and tied the end around my stick shift. Then I retracted the sun roof, angled the kite toward the sky, and set it free.

It flew. Maybe for only a minute or two, but oh how it whipped and oh how it soared and oh what a wild ride. More.

I tied two of the big carps to my wrists and got out of the car. The wind snapped them up in an instant. I could feel their protest, a moment's writhing defiance, then sudden surrender. I could feel the wind tugging at me, too, whispering promises in my ear. If I jumped, I wouldn't fall. I would fly with the carps and the fighter kites above the storm and across the ocean, to somewhere better and bigger and faster than this. I would dance with the devil any night that I chose. . . .

But I had promised the kites.

It took me almost an hour to set them all free, and by the time I was through I was sick to death of Melissa Etheridge's problems. I was cold and hungry and wet. It was miles still to Esalen, and hours after that until dinner. And they expected me to write in between. Write what. Write why. Thank God the car started and the appropriate lights stayed on and off, and nobody else was on the road to get in my way.

I must have been a scary sight at the Esalen gate, because the guard asked me for I.D. What the hell did he think I was going to do, anyway—crash a drum-beating class? He let me in without further argument. He even asked me if I was okay. Apparently nobody else had ventured off the grounds that day, because there wasn't an empty parking space within half a mile of my bungalow. It was a long, dreary trudge, carrying those heavy shopping bags through the mud, in the dark, without even a firefly to light the way. What had happened to the rain? What once felt like electric kisses against my skin now stung like whips across an open wound. And all that shouting, that unbearable shouting going on—the wind and the rain and the tormented trees, and the ocean bellowing up from below.

I didn't want quiet, but I didn't want this. I wanted my own noise, with nobody around to disturb it. I'll beat my own drums, I'll fly my own kite, and this is fair warning: Stay out of my way.

Something tugged at me when I passed by the glistening, manicured rock garden with its neat and certain border. There are people out there who don't want a wild ride on the wind, or to dance with the devil on a Saturday night. All they want is a careful garden that blossoms and withers according to season. For some people, there is enough. They don't have to want more, when more is nothing but more and is never enough.

I left my bags outside the bungalow door and went inside. I sat by the fire and towel-dried my hair. Minute by minute, it was the best I could do: stay tethered and wait out the storm.

12

I've never liked the telephone. It's a noisy, shrill
intruder. If it were up to me, I'd ban all phones and bring back
visiting days, like in Jane Austen and Edith Wharton novels:
"Ms. Cheney shall be in on Tuesday afternoons, from two to
four o'clock."

The entertainment lawyer is always in; it's part of the job
description. With the advent of voice mail, I lived in fear of the
blinking message light. It was always there, at the edge of my
desk, in the corner of my eye. But I just couldn't pick up the
phone. If I picked it up, I'd have to talk. If I talked, I'd have to
care. I was too depressed to pretend that I cared, too worn out
even to try.

Sick of playing hostage to a machine, I finally committed an unthinkable act. I stepped off the fast track, leaving my high-profile entertainment law firm to work part-time at a lesser known, though highly respectable, firm downtown. I'd like to say it was an act of courage, and maybe in part it was. But it was also an act of desperation. I simply couldn't take big-firm life anymore: the relentless pressure of the billable hour, the endless jockeying for favor, and most of all the scrutiny. I felt like I was being watched and judged every second of every waking hour, to see if I was partnership material.

Africa had changed me far more than I knew. I looked around at all the excesses of my Beverly Hills lifestyle and could no longer see them as badges of honor. I had so much, and yet I wanted more. I wanted to pursue that lifelong dream I'd confessed in my late-night talks with David. Crazy as it sounds, I wanted to write: a novel, not a screenplay, thank God, but still.

I was never happier.

Six months later I received a phone call from a lawyer I knew from the old days who was putting together what he called his "All-Star team" for a new sort of litigation specialty: Hollywood meets Silicon Valley. How could I resist? I was offered less hours for more money, at a firm I never dreamed would accept me as an associate. Once again, my business card would gain me entree into the hottest restaurants and the coolest clubs. I would belong. I looked over the hundred-plus pages of my beloved novel. It was nowhere near as compelling as that business card.

The new job wasn't so bad, really. It wasn't even such a bad life. It just wasn't *my* life, not anymore. I belonged again, but to everyone except myself. I sat at my nice, shiny mahogany desk all day, staring at the screaming phone. The six lines flashed in constant fits of impatience, and all I could do was stare back. What could they possibly want from me? Why couldn't I move? I managed to keep my condition a secret by coming in late at night and returning all the calls I hadn't answered that day. Sometimes I didn't even turn on the lights. I just sat in the dark, wondering why the next breath was necessary.

And then the Big Case slammed into my life, and I had no choice but to start acting like a lawyer who returned phone calls.

In every lawyer's life, there is a Big Case, maybe two. The bigger the firm, the bigger the case. But each is unique in the level of blood it sucks from your life. This case was a blood-sucker of the first magnitude. I knew, because it was the same Big Case I had escaped from when I'd left the fast track to go part-time. I had sidestepped this killer case by changing firms, only to have the client switch firms himself.

So here they all were again, Michael Jackson and the rest of the gang: the same agents, managers, lawyers, producers, record execs, and assorted starfuckers who had almost succeeded in drowning me before, with their constant demands and conflicting interests and relentless, unending, inexorable phone calls. Naturally, since I was intimately familiar with the cast of characters, I was assigned to the case, only a month before it was set for trial. Big celebrities almost never go to trial, but all attempts at settling this dispute had failed.

And so it began. One phone call had to be followed up by three, each of which required a fourth to confirm, with the message slips piling up exponentially. When a court date looms, every call is urgent. I couldn't return these phone calls from under my desk in the middle of night. It was trial time, and there was no day or night. Only deadlines.

I made it through the night. I always do. We won. We always do. When it was over, I took ten days off and stayed in a four-star bed and breakfast. I returned to the office knowing that my desk would be clean, the mahogany visible again, the telephone quiet. I smiled as I walked down the hall toward my office, confident that the insistent jangling I heard was for somebody else, some other poor slob caught up in the next Big Case.

When I opened my door, all six lights were flashing. Message slips were cascading off my chair to the floor. I picked one up: "Notice of appeal." I picked up a few more. "Urgent." "Appeal." "Call immediately." I swept the rest of the slips off my chair, sat down, and put my head on my desk. The lights kept blinking, the phone kept ringing, but I couldn't move my hand to pick it up. I knew it wouldn't make the noise go away. It would never go away. It would only be followed by the next noise, which might be even louder. Better just to sit there, quietly, my head on my desk, until it was time to go home.

The next day was the same, and the next, and the day after that—an intolerable accumulation, just like the papers piling up on my desk. I had one move left, the one I'd kept on hand in case of an emergency. One phone call. It was to Dr. R., the psychiatrist who promised that he could ease my pain if I would submit to a few months of electroconvulsive therapy—electroshock, or ECT, as it's known in the field. The decision to allow electrodes to be placed on each side of my skull, which would then transmit enough electrical voltage to send my body flying two feet off the operating table, was calm, almost lawyerlike in its logic. I had no other options left.

Dr. R. was considered one of the top diagnosticians in the United States, maybe even the world. His curriculum vitae stopped at twenty pages and just said, "Please call for further publications." Believe me, when he spoke, I listened. And all he said was, "ECT." The only possibility left was to try to shock the hell out of the depression.

So I signed the fifteen-page consent form. Three additional doctors had to assure Blue Cross that the treatment was necessary. After talking with me for twenty minutes, each doctor confirmed the need for immediate intervention. Dr. R. wrote in some kind of quasimedical diagnosis, so that my firm signed off on a three-month leave of absence. We all hoped that three months, twelve ECT sessions, and many thousands of dollars later, I would be well again. Better than well. I would be cured.

I remember almost nothing of the actual ECT, except the straps that bound me to the bed. They were thick, discolored with sweat, and they hurt. They left bruises on my arms and ankles for weeks after each session. I'm not sure that I *want* to remember the experience, although it makes for great dinner conversation. But whether I want to remember it or not is beside the point. The main side effect of ECT is that it wipes out your short-term memory. Some of it returns later, but for the most part, there are vast gray gaps in 1994. Despite the general fog, I still catch glimpses now and then, which may be true, or may only be fragments of a dream.

Ironically, the act of forgetting itself is very clear. I remember not being able to remember simple things, things I never even realized that I knew. The meaning of certain useless words, for example. The word *cornstarch* seemed particularly strange to me, and I still can't pass it in a supermarket without feeling a sense of dislocation. I also forgot the associations assigned to different colors. There seemed no functional distinction to me between red and green. (Fortunately, I was forbidden to drive while I was undergoing treatment.) I even forgot certain smells, like a snuffed-out candle, or Nivea hand cream—smells that had once been as familiar to me as my father's face. Which I also briefly forgot.

But mostly I remember the psychotic break that took place after my eighth ECT session, triggering the most severe manic episode of my life. Previous episodes had lasted several days in a row. This one lasted weeks. I've since learned that ECT can sometimes cause mania, even in a person who has never been manic before.

I may never be able to pin down in words the events of that nonstop twenty-four-hours-a-day, eighteen-day odyssey I embarked upon. What little I know of it, I pieced together through the sales receipts. I vaguely recall shooting up the coast to Big Sur to spend two weeks and an obscene amount of money for a tree house suite at the Post Ranch Inn. The management still sends me postcards of thanks, to this day. What I didn't spend on the Inn, I spent elsewhere, on anything that struck my fancy or satisfied my manic taste, which it turns out was very bad. I bought a dozen assorted garden gnomes, for example, even though I had no garden. By the time I came back home, I had not only gone through my entire savings account, I had seduced the husband of one dear friend and made plans to seduce another two evenings hence.

I don't know if it was the exhaustion of my neurotransmitters, my funds, or my sleep-deprived body, but I literally crashed when I came back to L.A. Ran smack into the cypress tree in front of my house. I saw it, of course. I knew it was there. But I felt like I was the stronger life force. Without my consciously willing it, my foot pushed down harder on the accelerator. I felt irresistibly drawn to go closer, and closer, without reducing my speed, to see if the tree would yield. It didn't.

My next ECT session—the ninth in the projected series of twelve—was scheduled for the following day. I unpacked as quickly as I could, laying out my clothes for the morning so that I could get an early start. I had to be at the hospital no later than five A.M. I remember only isolated parts of that morning. Dr. R. entered, and I started to tell him that things had been a bit, well, odd with me lately, but he was in his usual ultra-efficient rush. God, I admired that man's ability to cut a conversation short. That morning he seemed even more hurried than ever, a man with a mission: get this business over with. I chalked up the weird feelings I got from him to my weird feelings in general, and bit down on the thick wooden bar.

And then my world convulsed.

I remember very little of what happened over the next few

months. Only two things: first, Dr. R. was indicted for sexually molesting one of his patients, and his license was suspended; second, I tried to commit suicide. It's rather strange that I hadn't tried earlier, given the depth of my distress. But suicide requires movement, and depression weighs a thousand tons. I needed a spark of mania to quicken my step, to loosen my limbs, to fire up my resolve. Mania doesn't just give you the desire for extremes, it gives you the energy to pursue them. Race today, recoup tomorrow, if tomorrow ever comes.

Tomorrow meant nothing to me. Just more electrodes, more flashing phones, and a body that refused to move. I had more than enough drugs on hand, more than a hundred that would probably work. I know now that it's unusual for a doctor to allow a psychiatric patient to stockpile so many pills. But Dr. R., as always, followed his own rules. It turned out that in addition to molesting his patient, he was also indicted for flagrant abuse of his prescribing privileges. All the famous producers you've ever read about who overdosed on psychotropic meds—you can bet that Dr. R. was in their Rolodex.

I woke up in St. John's Hospital three days after my attempt, in a private padded room on the locked ward. Nobody told me about Dr. R.'s indictment, so I wondered why he wasn't there and hadn't called. I wondered why I was strapped down to the bed, since this wasn't the room where they did the ECT. Mostly, I wondered why I was still alive.

They tell me my exterminator found me. I love the irony of that. He comes once a month to spray for spiders. He has a key to my front door and enters at his own discretion. Instead of spiders, he found me, sprawled on the living room carpet, with blood and foam coming out of my mouth. I don't know what the foam was all about, maybe all the plastic capsules dissolving in the tequila. But the blood I understand: I bit halfway through my tongue. You've never discovered how loud you can scream until they give you twenty stitches in your tongue without an anesthetic.

Who knows what went wrong during that last ECT session? I personally think it was some strange kind of gift from the gods. I emerged from that chaos a different person, with a different identity. No longer depressed, but bipolar. The label mattered. It made sense of my erratic life. I had never before understood how, for several weeks or months at a time, I could function at such a high level of competence, only to be followed by equally long periods of hiding under my desk, under the covers, in the dark.

To be honest, I'd never really been comfortable with the concept of "depression," no matter how articulately I defended it to my family and friends. I had never disclosed my diagnosis to my colleagues. I still thought depression was something I should be able to control. God knows I'd heard it often enough—just pick yourself up by your bootstraps, or run five miles a day, or avoid all forms of sugar, and you could lick this thing. Everybody gets the blues.

But manic depression is just too crazy for most people to identify with, or have comforting platitudes for. There's a certain liberation in being so out there, beyond the norm. The layman rarely argues with you: your conduct speaks for itself. So I am genuinely insane every once in a while, but at least it's genuine insanity. It occupies a whole different space in the DSM-IV.

I'm still ashamed of having a mental illness. Perhaps I'll always be ashamed. But now it's mostly of the consequences, not the condition itself. I believe in this diagnosis. It's as true to me as being a redhead. Despite the constant shifting of the earth beneath my feet, I feel grounded at last.

13

My sins are greatest against those I never wished
to harm. Sins against the innocent never go unpunished,
and they always leave their mark. Look closely enough in the
mirror, and you'll see a whole new spate of crow's-feet, or a
crinkle in your forehead where it once lay smooth. To this day,
I see the furrows etched around my mouth, and all I can think
is: Linda.

Linda was the first real girlfriend I ever made in law
school. We bonded over a particularly sexist constitutional
law professor, who insisted on calling all his female students
"Missy." I was sick with depression most of the first semester;
and when I came back to class a few weeks before finals,

Linda voluntarily offered to lend me her notes. It was the first—and little did I know then—the only act of kindness I was ever to receive at UCLA Law. And it was the beginning of a friendship that lasted long past graduation, into the wilds of our professional careers.

Linda and I talked on the phone every day, sometimes two or three times if a crisis was in the offing. Crises ranged all the way from what do I wear to federal court to I think I'm falling in love with a senior partner. We shared shoes and sweaters, blind double dates, and even went bathing suit shopping together, which is surely the truest hallmark of intimacy and trust that can exist between two adult women.

I'd had girlfriends before, but it had been a long, long time since I'd felt this close and connected with another woman. All my other female friendships had gradually fallen to the wayside, one by one, as my manic depression got worse over time. I can hardly blame them: when I was depressed, I never returned phone calls. And when I was manic, I simply had no use for women. All I wanted to do was flirt, and flirting with women was no fun.

But Linda weathered the bipolar storms with patience and understanding. She didn't get angry with me when I was too depressed to call her back, or when I canceled long-standing plans over and over again. And while she didn't particularly like how I acted when I was manic, over time she learned how to handle that, too: she simply refused to go out in public with me. Instead, she would cook dinner at her house and we would rent old black-and-white movies, or she would come over to my place with her needlepoint and keep me company while I climbed the walls.

But Linda's tolerance was finally tested to the breaking point several years after law school, when I experienced a depression unlike any I had ever known before. It struck at the worst time possible, when I was under considerable professional strain, and also on the brink of being romantically involved with a senior partner at my new law firm. Night after night I called Linda and sobbed: How could I face another day of this? And she proved her friendship, again and again, by listening and not proffering advice.

"I can't move," I'd say. "All the gravity in the world is fixed on my body and it's pinning me down to the bed."

"I know," she'd answer, softly.

"I can't breathe," I'd say. "All the air in the world is being sucked out of my lungs and I don't have the strength to pull it back in again."

"I know," she'd say. "I know."

And so on and so on: I recited my endless litany of woes like a nightly confession, and she absolved me simply by breathing, calmly and gently, into the other end of the phone.

But like everything that is innately evil, the depression grew more loathsome with each passing day. Despair, until now shrill and pleading, grew quiet and crafty. I began to secretly fantasize about guns and knives and pills and nooses and open, empty veins. My nightly phone calls trickled down to three, then two, then one a week, at which point Linda became alarmed.

"You have to do something," she urged me one night. "I don't care what, or how much it costs, but you have to do something, *now*."

That's when I finally agreed to allow Dr. R. to perform electroshock therapy on my brain. Ultimately it was my decision, but in my mind I held Linda partly responsible, too. She had been so adamant, so convinced that twelve sessions of ECT, spread out over the next couple of months, would be the solution we had been praying for. She couldn't have known about the psychotic break it would trigger midway through the treatment, or the wild manic episode that followed that break, or my subsequent suicide attempt. All she knew was that I was suffering, and she wanted the pain to stop. ECT was the only way, she was sure.

Eventually, her confidence seemed justified. By the twelfth and final round of the ECT, I looked decidedly better. I was able to get up, get dressed, and groom myself. Although I wasn't sleeping much, it was enough so that the desperate, haunted look went out of my eyes. I could see the improvement myself in the mirror, but I was wary. The mirror couldn't show me my mind, and my mind felt decidedly strange.

The ECT may have kicked me out of the depression, but it kicked a little too hard. Not only did I lose most of my inhibitions, I lost a good part of my memory, too. I could remember some things well enough, usually arcane trivia like which of the Brontës wrote *Wuthering Heights*, but I completely forgot basic essential info like what different utensils were for. I happily ate my ice cream with a fork, my fish with a spoon. I forgot standard social etiquette, too, like the custom of shaking hands upon meeting someone. If they pleased me, I kissed them—full on the mouth. It's the only way I can explain what happened next: I forgot the very rules I was violating.

Linda was so happy at my apparent recovery that she decided to throw me a party, a "welcome back" party, as she called it. I hadn't socialized in almost a year, and I was just manic enough to long for an occasion—any occasion—to talk, to flirt, to express my opinions about everything under the sun. Linda was especially eager to introduce me to the brand-new man in her life: Jeff, an artist and photographer who taught art history on the side. "He's James Dean handsome," she whispered to me one night on the phone.

The party was on a steamy August night, and I was feverish with anticipation and mania. Linda's garden was tolerably comfortable, but nonetheless the guests all came dressed in as little clothing as possible. I had, of course, completely forgotten the contents of my wardrobe. So I'd assembled an outfit out of disparate odds and ends: a lovely white silk scarf that I fashioned as a halter top, and a brightly checkered red-and-white sarong that might have been a tablecloth in my pre-ECT existence.

I thought I looked fabulous. But then I thought everyone and everything looked fabulous that night: Linda, the other guests, the cunning little carved ivory napkin holders, the tuna carpaccio canapés. I was acutely aware of the extent of exposed flesh all around me—not just my own, but the other women's—and it suddenly seemed to me the most natural thing in the world. I'd never realized until that moment how much of the world is naked under the bare-ass moon.

What a difference a few months had made. Before the ECT, the world had been a dull and muddy gray, with strains of funereal black. Now it was raucous and bright as a tropical parrot, and just as exotic. I seemed to hear things I'd never really heard before: one leaf rustling up against another, the insinuating whisper of the wind. And the smells . . . I closed my eyes and inhaled the night-blooming jasmine so deeply I got giddy. I staggered back a few steps and tripped over the dinner table, falling to my knees and sending an assortment of silverware clattering to the ground.

"Gravity is conspiring against you," I heard a voice say, and when I opened my eyes there was Linda's James Dean, smiling down at me. He held out his hand. "You must be Terri," he said. "Linda never told me how graceful you were." I reached up and took his outstretched hand, aware all at once of a surge of heat passing between our palms.

"Thank you," I said, discreetly adjusting my sarong. "But I don't believe in gravity." Which was true. Since the ECT, natural laws no longer existed for me.

He asked me what I had meant, and I explained myself, carelessly. I knew the particular words I used didn't matter. What mattered was the sound of my voice, snaking into his ear. Besides, he wasn't really listening, just looking at me—staring, in fact. He interrupted me: "Has anyone ever told you that you look just like Vermeer's *Girl with a Pearl Earring*? The high forehead, the round face, the pale lashes and brows . . ."

Damn the ECT. I remembered Vermeer, but for the life

of me I couldn't recall his *Girl with a Pearl Earring*. But all Vermeer's women were lovely, I thought, so I decided to take a chance that the remark was a compliment.

"Thank you?" I said, with a rising inflection.

"In fact, I'd really like to photograph you one of these days," Jeff said, and there it was: the unmistakable declaration. He was interested, and I—I was half a dozen different emotions at once. Flustered, flattered, triumphant, shy, excited and lascivious. Definitely lascivious. Due to the depression, it had been at least a year since I'd had sex.

"Yes" was on my lips and inches away from the air when a small, nagging doubt seized hold of me. Something was wrong here, terribly wrong, but what that thing was I just couldn't remember. He was gorgeous, I was available, what else mattered? And this is where I plead to God to consider the mitigating circumstances: that between the mania-induced lust and the ECT-induced amnesia, I honestly forgot that there was anything more essential at stake, i.e., the unwritten rules of friendship. In particular, Rule No. One: stay away from your best friend's boyfriend. I took a good long look at Jeff's gold-flecked eyes and Roman nose and chose to believe in the law of the moment.

"I'd love to," I said. "When did you have in mind?"

We spent the rest of that evening not ten feet apart (Linda had thoughtfully seated us next to each other at the table). Somewhere between the vichyssoise and the cold poached salmon, the guilt finally hit me. But by then I was too deep into the flirtation to get myself out of it. Nor, I will admit it now, did I really want to. For the first time in ages, I felt alive. I knew, without articulating it into words, that this was what life was really about, that this was what we are here for: to seduce and be seduced.

By the time the party finally broke up, an hour or so after midnight, Jeff had my telephone number and we had made a date to get together tomorrow at his studio. I didn't, of course, tell Linda about this, either that night or the morning after, when she called to rehash the party with me. "So what did you think of Jeff?" she asked. "Nice," I replied, then I quickly changed the subject. I could tell she was a little bit miffed, but I didn't trust myself.

When I finally managed to hang up the phone, a good hour later, I was thoroughly exasperated with Linda for making me feel guilty when I hadn't done anything yet. Plus she had completely fouled up my schedule: I was supposed to meet Jeff at his studio at one o'clock, and here it was already a quarter past twelve. I tore through my closet, quickly trying on and discarding a half dozen outfits before settling on a pale pink sweater and jeans. The sweater had a flattering sweetheart neckline with white eyelet trim: it clothed me in innocence. To look at me, you'd never know what I was really thinking.

Being both manic *and* in a hurry is hardly conducive to good driving. I sped down the hill at twice the speed limit, honking my horn all the way through the intersections. My mind was racing far ahead of my car: what would I do if and when Jeff actually tried to touch me? I didn't know the answer. I couldn't get past the moment of contact. How lovely it would feel to be touched again by any man, but especially by Jeff.

I arrived at the studio intact and on time. I knocked on the door and within a few seconds, Jeff answered. He was even more handsome by daylight. The whites of his eyes were even brighter against his dark tan, and traces of silver shot through his hair. He ushered me in and led me to the kitchen, where a pitcher of margaritas lay waiting on a tray, with two frosted and salt-rimmed glasses. How could he have possibly known? When I'm manic, tequila is always my drink of choice. The only problem is, tequila exacerbates every urge. The tiniest flicker of mania becomes a full-blown fire.

I hesitated for just a second or two before wrapping my fingers around the ice-cold glass. Ignoring all echoes of reason and restraint, I slowly, deliberately thrust out my tongue and lightly traced the salt-flecked rim, my eyes fixed on Jeff's all the while. "Bring your glass," he said, and he led me down the hall into his studio proper, a large, barren room with a cathedral ceiling, enormous skylights and a bank of mirrors all along the back wall. "It used to be a dance hall," he explained, waving a hand toward the mirrors. "Now I use them for trick shots and special effects." He sat me down on a three-legged stool, facing the mirrors. Then he spent a few minutes adjusting the lights, before he finally looked at me through a small, hand-held camera. "What do you want me to do?" I asked, suddenly nervous and shy. "Do nothing," he said. "Just look in the mirror and think Vermeer."

So I looked in the mirror and thought Vermeer. But the image staring back at me looked nothing like his women: calm, serene, and eternally still. The woman in the mirror fidgeted; she was restless; her eyes kept darting back and forth. I was exceedingly ill at ease, uncomfortable in my own skin.

"Stop fidgeting," Jeff said. He set his camera down, walked up to my stool and gently smoothed my hair down with his fingers. I was still staring into the mirror, and at the instant he touched me, I could see myself shiver. Apparently Jeff could feel it, too, because he turned around and looked up. Just for a moment, our eyes met and locked in the mirror.

And that's when I knew: I owed my dear friend Linda allegiance, but I owed the woman in the mirror something more. It was a miracle that I was still alive, after a year of bone-crushing, soul-starving depression. It was a miracle my brain still functioned well enough to flirt. I thought back to the face I'd seen in my bathroom mirror before the ECT: sullen, sallow, the smile muscles slack from disuse. And I looked at me now: pink-cheeked and blooming, trembling with anticipation, every pore, every freckle alive and alert.

Funny, I thought, I never pictured myself as one of "those" women—one of those heartless harpies who could steal a man right from under her best friend's nose. But try as I might, I just couldn't feel guilty. Much as I loved Linda, I realized now that my loyalties lay elsewhere. I owed it to myself to snatch at happiness however I could. Who knew when or if it would come again?

I reached up and stroked Jeff's cheek with my finger. He leaned down and kissed me once on each eyelid, then on my forehead, then on the tip of my nose, hovering just above my lips until I finally couldn't stand the tension a second longer. I grabbed the back of his neck and kissed him long and hard.

And so it became part of our relationship mythology that I kissed him first. Hence I was responsible for breaking whatever vows either of us may have owed to Linda. I questioned this reasoning, at least at first: even assuming *arguendo* that I was the seducer, wasn't he also at fault for being seduced? Shouldn't he have been more cautious, more wary? Or did part of him really want to be caught? Jeff invariably shrugged off these questions with an exasperated sigh. What's done is done, he said. You dwell too much on the past.

He was wrong. If I dwelled on anything, it was the future, my future with Jeff, to be exact. I knew deep down that I had committed an unpardonable sin, and the only way that I could live with that fact was to somehow keep the sin alive. So I refused to settle for a one-night stand. I did everything in my power to make Jeff care. Fortunately, the mania helped: I was charming and vivacious in spite of myself. I didn't tell Jeff about being bipolar, he knew nothing about the ECT, and he was just smitten enough in our early affair to find my frequent memory lapses an adorable quirk.

A week, two weeks, a month went by, and Jeff and I grew closer every day. In all this time, I never once mentioned his name to Linda. She, however, kept bringing him up. She couldn't understand why he had suddenly pulled away. "He just stopped calling me out of the blue," she'd tell me, over and over again. "I can't understand it. I really thought that he might be the one." I'd murmur sympathetically, then talk of other things. But every day the guilt grew worse. I began to dread the telephone, knowing that more likely than not the caller would be Linda, asking her eternal why. So I started answering less and less, until eventually our conversations dwindled down to once a week, then once a fortnight, then once a month, then not at all. I pleaded every excuse I could possibly think of to justify my silence: out-of-town visitors, a heavy workload, a recurrence of depression, the flu. But never once did I mention the actual truth: that I was falling in love.

Because it *had* to be love, I told myself. I wasn't the kind of girl who would betray her best friend for anything less. So I overlooked Jeff's many flaws: his clumsy little lies, his soggy kisses, his penchant for talking out loud in movies and wearing woolen socks to bed. And when, four months into our relationship, he had a quickie with a cocktail waitress, I ignored that, too. I figured it was just as much my fault as his. My mania had reached the irritable stage by then, and I'd been quarrelsome and bitchy to everyone, but especially to Jeff.

I couldn't help it. Just beneath the surface prickliness lay a deep and tender wound, a constant, aching loneliness. I'd try to talk to Jeff about my day at work, about opposing counsel's tacky shoes, for example, or an awkward elevator moment with a senior partner, but the most I would get was a cursory nod. Or worse yet, he would offer me earnest advice on how to fix the problem.

"I don't want advice," I tried explaining one night over dinner.

"Then why are you complaining?" he asked me, spearing an asparagus shoot with his fork.

"I'm not complaining," I replied. "I'm . . . well, I'm . . ." But it was hopeless. I gave up and stuffed my mouth with an enormous bite of mu-shu pork. The truth was, damn it, I *was* complaining. But somehow it hadn't seemed like that when I used to talk to Linda.

That night I lay awake long after Jeff had fallen asleep. I stared at the doors, the skylights, the windows: so many possible means of escape. I pulled back the sheet, gently so as not to awaken him, and examined Jeff's body. It was a beautiful body, hard and lean, and it had given me many hours of pleasure. But the illicit thrill we had both felt at first, when we were so acutely aware of cheating on Linda, had disappeared. It was replaced by a low, steady heat, still intensely enjoyable, but lacking the wicked lure of hellfire.

I lay back and stared at the ceiling. After all the hours I had spent in Catholic school studying sin, you'd think that I would understand it better. But I hadn't realized that after that first delicious plunge into temptation, you just keep falling, and falling, and falling forever. Gravity not only exists, it seems. It is a moral imperative. And it was going to keep me bound to this man, locked in an endless free-fall together, for as long as he would have me, for as long as I could convince him to stay.

Which is exactly what ended up happening. Jeff and I remained friends, and are friends to this day. We'll always be friends, or lovers, or something else inextricably entwined. It's not about love, it's about retribution. When God wants to punish us, he grants us our sins.

14

I'd never hit a man before. I was surprised how
good I was at it. The anger had been building up all week, and
I couldn't quite make sense of it. Nothing was wrong, really,
nothing that I could point to. In fact, everything looked pretty
damned good on the surface: after years of being on-again,
off-again lovers, Rick and I were back together. He was treating
me to a vacation at my favorite spot on earth, Big Sur. Our
top-floor suite had a wraparound view of the sea. All week
long, I had slow, sensual massages. I was stroked and sloughed,
wrapped in seaweed, drenched in oils. It was all too much: the
perfect coastline, the generous boyfriend, the ideal vacation. I
squirmed beneath the masseuse's gentle fingers. "Too hard?"

she asked. "Too much," I mumbled unintelligibly into the face pad.

There was no use trying to explain it to her, to Rick, or to anyone else—not until I had figured it out for myself. Less than a month before, I had been in a desperate depression, so bleak, so utterly hopeless that killing myself seemed the only solution that made any sense. Night after night I dreamed about suicide. But much as I wanted to take those pills or tie that noose, I couldn't. My body simply refused to obey my mind's commands. I just lay there—unwashed, uncombed, and drowning in inertia, struggling with the need to breathe in and out. But irony apparently thrives in depression, because the paralysis is no doubt what kept me alive. Had I been able to move the least little bit, I would surely have seized the first chance to die.

Like most of my chemical depressions, this one came all of a sudden, out of the blue, like a freak electrical storm in the middle of a sunny summer afternoon. My recovery was just as unpredictable. Early one otherwise unremarkable morning, I woke up to find the sun shining straight into my eyes. I lay there in discomfort a few moments, and then rolled over to the other side of the bed, not realizing the significance of this simple gesture. For the first time in weeks, my body had actually executed a direct command from my brain. "Get out of the sun, you fool." And I did.

Little by little, breathing became autonomous again, an invisible companion I quickly came to accept and ignore. I even found myself answering the telephone now and then. At first, of course, I merely picked up the ringing receiver and stared at it, awed at my newfound capacity to move. But eventually, I held the phone all the way up to my ear and even spoke a few words in reply. It seems an absurdly simple thing, perhaps, hardly cause for fanfare. But anyone who knows severe depression, or me, knows that talking on the phone means the worst is surely past. The paramedics won't have to be called tonight. Suicide watch is over, for now.

Everyone in my life rejoiced, and none more so than Rick, who had called so often without the hope of my ever returning the call. It made sense when Rick called me up late one night a few weeks later, his voice a little thick with wine, to propose a recovery celebration. "We've earned it," he said, and I smiled at the "we." "Ten days in Big Sur, on me. You don't have to do anything but lie back and commune with the trees. It'll do you more good than all those goddamned drugs put together."

My medication was always a thorny subject between us: Rick reluctantly acknowledged the need for me to be on some kind of mood stabilizer, but he never fully approved of the number and variety of drugs I had to take on a daily basis. "It's polypharmacology," I used to try to explain. "It's pill-popping" was his reply. We had learned to leave it at that. I ignored it and moved on to the trip: where would we stay, when would we go, how would we get there.

Not that I really cared about any of this. I was perfectly happy to let Rick handle all the details. That was what Rick did best in our relationship: he handled the details. He took care of things—meaning, mostly, he took care of me. Did I have enough food in the house? Were my utilities paid this month? When would my dry cleaning be ready? Whatever it was, Rick saw to it: all the bills, all the bother.

It hadn't always been like this. When we first met, in college, I was adamantly self-sufficient. I was a Vassar girl, I was no man's obligation. But my disease was only intermittently disabling then. Bad as the depressions were, they didn't last as long, or recur as often, and the periods in between were flush with promise. Over the next ten years, as the illness grew progressively worse and harder to hide, independence became more than a rallying cry, it became an obsession. I lived in terror of being found out, and fortunately, independence was a handy façade for a young career woman.

At least, I called it independence. The men in my life had other names for it, few of them complimentary. I kept them all at bay, as far in the dark and as far from my heart as possible, even Rick, who knew me best and probably loved me most. We continued to date off and on for almost ten years after college, at which point he left in frustration, and I retreated further behind my stony wall of self-reliance.

Self-reliance failed me soon after my father's death. I was sick. I was broke. I needed to eat. I needed help. It was useless to try to pretend otherwise. I picked up the phone and dialed those seven digits I thought I had long since put to rest. I cried, and begged for help, and Rick came to me.

For months afterward, the slightest demand on my nerves sent me spiraling into hysteria and deeper depression. Rick saw it all, and to my surprise was not repulsed. He was moved to help. The first time he offered me money, I outright refused. The next time, I protested for a couple of days, then reluctantly accepted. Eventually my protests became shorter and fewer, until one day I forgot to say anything at all except "Thank you."

And so Rick gradually took over the minutiae of my life, all those desperate little details that were simply beyond my ability to handle.

Rick and his details. I was suddenly filled with affection for him, listening to the sound of his voice on the phone, eagerly reciting the itinerary of our proposed trip. God, I was lucky to have a man like him in my life. And how wonderful to go to Big Sur together. It would be just what I needed, the perfect vacation, except . . .

Except.

I knew I should have been chiming in with enthusiasm, asking questions, offering suggestions. But depression, like any virulent poison, doesn't just exit your system all at once. It lingers in pockets and traces, long after you think you've recovered. Even at that moment, I could feel myself stiffening at the mere thought of packing. So many decisions to make: Which pair of evening shoes, or any at all? Black jeans or blue jeans, and how many sweaters? SPF 15 or 30? Or 45, just in case?

The mere fact that I was holding the telephone meant something, I reminded myself. It meant that I was getting better, and that the business of life was upon me again. It was time to take chances, to make up for lost momentum, to move forward.

"I'd love to," I said, interrupting Rick's spiel. "What time should I be ready?"

The drive up to Big Sur was sublime, the hills along Pacific Coast Highway a rolling carpet of color. I wanted to stop to pick wildflowers along the way, and I chose to ignore my irritation when Rick said he'd buy me some at the hotel instead. But by the time we arrived, it was long past sunset. Too late for store-bought flowers, too late for cocktails on the terrace, too late for anything but bed. I wasn't sleepy, but I felt strange: restless and edgy. While I was unpacking, Rick crept up behind me and nuzzled my neck. I jerked away.

"It's not you," I tried to explain. "It's just . . . I don't know. I don't want to be touched."

I saw a flash of hurt and disappointment in his eyes. Then he smiled. "You need your flowers," he said. "I'll call the concierge first thing in the morning."

"Rick, it's not the flowers. It's me. I feel funny. Prickly, irritable. Like I'm depressed, but I can still move."

I saw him start at the word *depressed*. "You're just tired," he said. "I'll draw you a bath." And he turned away and headed into the bathroom.

It was a magnificent bath, I have to admit. I lay there with my eyes closed, willing my body to relax and my mind to empty. But the pressure of the warm, soapy water against my skin was unbearable. I sat up and flicked off the Jacuzzi switch, only to be assaulted by waves of bubbles. Bubbles, bubbles everywhere: in my face, up my nose, in my hair. I forced myself to slide back down into the water and lie there completely still until every last bubble had evaporated. Then I counted slowly up to one hundred, listening for any noises coming from the bedroom. Rick was a sound sleeper. If I could just endure waiting in the tub until after he'd gone to bed, I could slip in under the covers and he would never even know I was there until morning.

Morning. Would he still want to touch me then? Would I still feel untouchable? The morning would just have to wait, I decided. My fingers and toes were pruny from overexposure, and the water had long since turned chilly and flat. I stepped out of the tub as quietly as I could, wrapping several thick towels around me to catch any drips. Then I shut off the light and carefully eased open the bathroom door. No signs of life, just an inert form on Rick's side of the bed. I dropped the towels to the floor and tiptoed across the bedroom, sliding noiselessly under the covers.

The satin sheets felt like sandpaper against my flesh, and the tick-tock of the bedside clock sounded ominously like a waiting bomb. Rick mumbled something and rolled over in my direction. I moved just before our bodies touched, and then nestled my pillow into the curve of his stomach. It worked. He grew quiet again. Resisting the guilty urge to kiss his sleeping cheek, I retreated to the other room—thankful that Rick always insisted on suites.

I woke up early the next morning full of energy, eager to go, and irritable as a drenched cat. Everything Rick did annoyed me, from the way he tapped each side of his soft-boiled egg six times precisely, to the way he said "love you," without the "I." He said "love you" a lot those next few days. In fact, the more annoyed I became, the more affectionate he became. I continued to sleep on the living room sofa, but Rick didn't say a word about it. The issue of unfulfilled sex hung in the air between us. Rick insisted that I get a massage every afternoon, even though I told him I still didn't want to be touched. After five days I finally put my foot down. I didn't want a massage that afternoon, I wanted to go into town, alone. By myself. "Without you," I added for emphasis.

Rick didn't like the idea, but he let me go after making me promise that I'd be back in time for dinner. I wanted to go everywhere and see everything, but for the life of me I didn't know what I actually wanted to do. There were too many options, plus the rental car smelled funny and I couldn't get the damned air-conditioning right. Out of habit, I headed for a nearby bookstore, only to be bombarded with the eager smiles of salespeople, all wanting my attention. I couldn't understand it. This used to be one of my favorite bookstores ever. I had spent dozens of happy hours in here, perusing the shelves, chatting with the knowledgeable, if quirky, clerks. When did it all become so hateful—or was the real question, when did I become so full of hate?

Reluctantly, I bypassed the superlative Sherlock Holmes collection and headed toward the mental health section. Kicking the resident cat off a big, overstuffed chair, I gathered up several armloads of books and settled in to read. Something was wrong with me, I suspected; I just didn't have the name for it yet. I hated the world, I hated myself, and dying sounded just fine to me: all classic symptoms of depression. But—and it was a crucial but—I could still move. Not only *could* I move, I *had* to move. I was full of restless, undissipated energy that had no place to go, making me want to strike out and break something, preferably something that would crash and tinkle into a thousand satisfying tiny pieces. I thought of our hotel room with the wraparound picture window view, and it suddenly made sense: no wonder I couldn't enjoy the massages. The entire time, I'd been fantasizing about how it would feel to take my fist and smash all that glass, smash it over and over again until nothing remained but a heap of shards.

It took me a few more hours, and several more books, but I finally found it: the solution to the mystery, the clinical term for what was wrong with me. Apparently there's a strange place on the bipolar spectrum called a "mixed state," in which mania and depression meet and collide. In a mixed state, you have all the relentless, agitated drive of mania, but none of the euphoria. Instead, you feel depression's misery and self-loathing. It's the most dangerous condition possible, the one in which the most suicides occur. No longer protected by depression's inertia, you now have the ability to act upon your despair.

There it was, in black and white: my absolution. I wasn't crazy. It wasn't depression, it wasn't even mania. It was a mixed state. I was entitled to feel horrible, it was a mixed state. I kept saying the term over and over to myself on the way back to the hotel, to make it real. For the first time since our trip began, I couldn't wait to see Rick, to tell him all about it.

My research had taken much longer than I expected, and I arrived at the hotel half an hour later than I had promised. Rick was cross, and trying hard not to show it. But I knew his smile far too well to be fooled by indulgent imitations. I kissed his cheek and ruffled his hair, the first spontaneous gestures of affection I had exhibited in weeks. "You can stop trying not to scowl now," I said. "It's going to be okay. I know what's wrong. It's called a mixed state." I explained it to him as best I could. "So you see, that's why I've been acting so funny. It's like I'm depressed, except I'm manic, too. So you can understand why . . ."

He interrupted me. "You're not depressed. You're better. You're just exhausted from everything you've been through lately. Why don't we stay in tonight and relax? Here, let me fix you a drink."

"I don't want a drink," I replied. "I want to talk about this."

"Not now," Rick said. "You're too tired. You should have kept the appointment with the masseuse instead of spending all afternoon grubbing around in a bookstore."

I could feel my hands beginning to clench, the fingernails pressing into the flesh of my palms. The bite felt good. I pressed harder, trying to distract myself from the anger that was steadily building inside me.

Rick mistook my silence for acquiescence. He picked up the telephone and dialed room service. "I know just what you need," he said. "A good, thick steak with mashed potatoes on the side—or maybe some creamed spinach instead, for the iron. Which would you prefer?"

"I'd prefer that you put the goddamned phone down and listen to what I'm trying to say."

"I heard you," he said. "I'm just trying to fix it."

I crossed the room and took the phone out of his hand. My voice came out sounding curt and strangled, a good half-octave higher than normal.

"Sometimes it just can't be fixed, Rick. It's a disease. For once, stop trying to make it better and just let it be. Just ask me where it hurts."

We stared at each other, the tension rising between us

like heat. I could feel it on my skin, a prickly wave of fear and irritation. And I could see it reflected in Rick's stormy eyes: the moment we'd both been avoiding for years.

"Admit it, Rick," I insisted. "Sometimes it just can't be fixed, not even by you."

Rick reached down behind me and picked up the phone. His eyes were still defiant, but his voice was deadly calm. "Mashed potatoes or creamed spinach?"

And so I hit him. I reached back into years of pent-up anger and resentment, years of pretending to be all better because better was what Rick had bought and paid for, because he was the fixer and I the fixee, and better was part of the bargain. I reached way back and I hit him with all the force I could muster, square on the chin. This was no movie star slap. It was a bare-bones wallop—so hard that he staggered backward and would have fallen if the sofa hadn't come to his rescue, so hard that I broke the skin on two of my knuckles.

I hit him so hard that for a moment—for one moment only, but it was enough—the history between us was knocked awry, and we stood facing each other like two strangers in absolute silence. Then remorse rushed in, and I burst into tears and tried to throw myself into his arms. But he refused to hold me. He refused even to look at me. He just sat there, motionless, staring up at the ceiling as I cried.

"It's not me," I pleaded. "It's this bizarre mixed state. All week long I've been feeling a desperate need to hit something. It's almost overwhelming. I can't explain it. But I never meant for it to be you. Please, please say you understand."

"Okay, I understand," he said, still staring at the ceiling.

"Then you forgive me?" I asked.

"I forgive you," he said.

"And it's all okay?"

He finally looked down at me. "You know, sometimes it just can't be fixed," he said. Then he stood up, walked into the bedroom, and began to pack.

I didn't know it at the time, but that was our last conversation. True to form, Rick arranged all the details to see that I got home safely, but when I arrived, it was to an empty house and a silent phone.

It took ten days for the skin on my knuckles to heal. By that time, the mixed state had passed and I was back on the familiar ground of plain old depression. Every time I looked at the wound above my ring finger, I was overwhelmed by shame. I couldn't fathom how I—the great pacifist—could have done it, especially to Rick, who was no doubt the great love of my life. For months, I stared at that small raised reminder and despaired of ever understanding, much less forgiving, myself.

And then it struck again: the strange agitation, coupled with a despondence so profound I felt like I could barely breathe. The only thing that helped relieve my discomfort was the sound of breaking glass, and I smashed half-a-dozen teacups before it dawned on me that this, too, was familiar ground. But it took several more episodes before I really began to comprehend the mixed state's awesome power of destruction. Few things are strong enough to survive that deadly clash of mania and depression. Certainly not love. Love is far too fragile: it is a picture window, just begging to be shattered.

15

It's impossible, in my opinion, to have a normal relationship with food if you're manic-depressive. I have a theory: the disease significantly impairs the hypothalamus, which is the part of the brain that regulates appetite. But I don't need theories to prove my point. The empirical evidence, in my case at least, is overwhelming. For as far back as I can remember, food has always been inextricably linked to mood.

It's been ages since I've eaten a simple sandwich—longer still since I've swallowed an entire meal. There's no one simple reason I can give you as to why I can't eat like a normal human being. There are dozens of reasons, actually, but in the end there are none. It's an inexplicable phenomena. I really don't know why, after years of steady abuse, my body finally chose this moment in my early forties to fall spectacularly apart. Suffice to say, my body now treats food like a foreign invader. Only minuscule amounts are allowed to enter before the entire system goes on the attack. One bite too many, and my stomach suddenly swells to such an enormous girth that strangers eye me anxiously and ask when I am due. And then the pains begin: sharp, shooting stabs all along my lower abdomen, so intense they make me shiver uncontrollably and cry out loud for help.

But there's no help, and I already know it. I've seen all the doctors, taken all their tests, swallowed their pills, and listened to them, one after another, give up. The colon, it appears, is a mysterious and powerful being: easily provoked but incredibly hard to appease, not unlike an ancient tribal god. Which finally makes sense. Because what we are dealing with, when all is said and done, is the primal curse of manic depression.

Although I had noticeable mood swings throughout my early childhood, I didn't experience my first really, truly suicidal depression until I was sixteen years old. For well over a month, I slept twenty to twenty-two hours per day: fitful, dream-riddled slumber that left me even more exhausted. When I finally woke, I ate—and that's all I did. I didn't go to school; I didn't talk to family or friends; I didn't even read, which was the biggest loss. But I didn't care. Nothing mattered to me anymore but the consummate frenzy of hand-to-mouth, hand-to-mouth feeding.

I never stopped to ask myself why I was so hungry. All

I knew was that as long as I was engaged in the process of chewing and swallowing, I didn't think about anything else. Sensation completely replaced emotion. I didn't feel anything more complex than salty or sweet, smooth or crunchy. And I didn't give a damn about anything beyond the next bite.

Nor did I care what I was actually putting into my mouth. At first the food was fairly normal, although in increasingly large amounts: mashed potatoes, baby-backed ribs, leftover meatloaf, and mounds of spaghetti—whatever was in the refrigerator that night and relatively easy to prepare. But pretty soon I became too ravenous to wait for the food to heat up. I entered my raw stage, eating all the fruits and vegetables in the crisper. Cereal was quicker without the milk. Rice and pasta were a whole lot faster without the water, too.

My mother went grocery shopping one day a week, usually on Sunday, so by Friday we'd be almost completely out of food. I clearly remember those endless Friday nights when there was nothing left in the cupboard and depression was gnawing a hole in my stomach. I had to eat something, anything. Toward the end of my depression, I ate whatever was there: iced coffee packets, bags of flour, spices ranging from anise to fennel to marjoram to thyme. Of course my body eventually rebelled and I wound up throwing up half of what I frantically shoved down my throat. I didn't stop until I finally fell asleep, exhausted, with my hand still clutching whatever I was eating.

My father finally found me late one night, sprawled out across the living room sofa, too sick to move. I'd just consumed an entire box of baking soda, and I was lying there trying to muster the strength to get up and vomit. "I heard a noise . . . "

my father said, then he stopped short when he saw the white powder on my face, and the empty box of baking soda lying on the pillow. "What the hell?" he said, and the sound of his voice made me shrink with shame. "Honey, look at me," he pleaded; and perhaps it was the "honey" or the tenderness of his tone, but with his words, my body came back into being. And with it came all the feelings I had been trying so hard to suppress.

I grabbed my father's hand and looked up at him through a sudden flood of tears. "Daddy, I've lost control," I whispered, the first time in my life that I had ever admitted that to anyone, most importantly myself. I told him all about the food, about the raging hunger. I even told him what I feared the most: that mouthful by mouthful, bite by bite, I was steadily devouring my sanity.

My father had just recently stopped smoking, so he knew a thing or two about the inner demons of appetite. He squeezed my hand and reassured me that if he could stop smoking, I could certainly stop eating. But it would take a little outside help, and he knew just the place to get it.

Daddy had conquered his nicotine cravings with the help of an outfit named the Schott Center, which was all the rage in the mid-1970s. Controversy clung to the Schott Center, but I didn't know why. All I knew from the brochures that my father had brought home was that it was a behavioral modification program for the treatment of smoking and obesity—but what that entailed, I had no clear idea. My father hadn't told me much about his own experience, but that was nothing new. Daddy was never much of a talker. For him, actions were more important than words.

By nine A.M. the following morning, Daddy had already enrolled me in the Schott Center's obesity program. He insisted on driving me himself. At first I was grateful for the moral support, but by the third freeway interchange I'd undergone a total change of heart.

"This is stupid," I said. "Turn the car around."

My father continued to whistle "You Are My Sunshine" through the gap in his two front teeth.

"I'm not obese," I argued. Which was certainly true. I had inherited my mother's small frame and quick metabolism. Sopping wet and in my stocking feet, I stood five feet five inches and weighed an average of one hundred and ten pounds. Granted, the past few months of nonstop eating had packed a few extra inches on my stomach and thighs, but no one would call me obese.

"This is not about your weight," my father countered. "It's about control."

We pulled off the freeway, rounded a corner, and stopped in front of a small, nondescript gray building. "This is it," he said. "I'll be waiting here for you when you get out."

"You're not coming in with me?"

"I think this is something you need to do for yourself," he said, and then he leaned over and gave me a kiss on the cheek. I waited for the magic words, our secret battle cry, and I wasn't disappointed. "Give 'em hell, baby," my father said.

It was just as I thought: I was the only thin person in the waiting room. I quickly gave my name to the zaftig receptionist, then I buried myself in a promotional brochure, trying hard not to notice the curious and, in a few cases, downright hostile looks that kept coming my way. Fortunately, I didn't have to wait very long before a young man dressed all in white came to fetch me.

"I'm Joe," he said. "I'll be your counselor today." He led me into a small, dimly lit room furnished with two chairs, a sink, and a table. On top of the table was an assortment of foods, ranging from potato chips to cheese to bagels to salami, plus a wide variety of desserts, from muffins to Twinkies to what looked like some seriously tasty cookies.

Joe waved his hand over the spread. "Pick your very favorite," he said. "The one you can least resist."

No contest there. I'd already started salivating at the sight of the oatmeal raisin cookies. These looked like the really good kind, too—lacy crisp at the edges and soft and doughy in the center, with just the right amount of raisins. Joe noticed where my eyes had landed. "So it's oatmeal raisin cookies, is it?" he asked. "That's excellent." Then he piled five cookies on a small paper plate, handed them to me, and directed me to sit down in front of the sink.

"I want you to close your eyes now, take a big bite of cookie, and chew," Joe ordered. I did what he said, or at least I tried to comply, but the moment I bit down into the cookie I felt like I had been hit by lightning. I opened my eyes, and saw Joe grinning down at me with a long metal stick in his hand.

"It's along the same principles as your standard-issue cattle prod," he told me, waving the metallic wand in the air. "But it doesn't leave a mark. Now take another bite and chew—but don't swallow."

I bit, I chewed, and zap! another jolt of electricity shot

through me. "Now spit it all out into the sink," Joe said. I was embarrassed but willing. I spat out a wad of half-masticated cookie.

"Look at it. Touch it. What does it remind you of?" Joe asked me. Chewed-up cookie, was all that came to my mind.

"No, really look at it," Joe commanded. "Dig your fingers in there deep. Smell it. Lick it. Roll it around on your tongue. You know what it reminds me of? Poo-poo diapers. Baby shit. That's what you've been stuffing your face with all this time. Baby shit." Then he zapped me several times in a row.

Now I realized what the brochure's vague reference to "aversion therapy" had meant. The only problem was, I wasn't developing any aversion whatsoever to oatmeal raisin cookies. Rather, I was developing a serious aversion to the Schott Center itself: to that dimly lit cubicle, that gleaming, stainless-steel sink, and most especially to that grinning idiot Joe, with his cheery scatological chatter and mega-watt stick.

The rest of that afternoon went by in a blur. I chewed up and spat out four more of the cookies, and was forced to swallow several mouthfuls of regurgitated mess. I did whatever Joe asked me to do, hoping to somehow avoid or lessen the shocks. But the more compliant I became, the more shocks I received. There was simply no logic to it. I, who had always done so well on tests, could not seem to please this teacher at all. By the time I left, I was fighting back tears.

That was the end of my ill-fated experiment with the Schott Center, but not the end of my troubles with food. Fortunately, the depression that devastated my sixteenth year did not last forever. When it lifted, so did my abnormal cravings and hunger, for a while at least. They returned in full force with my next depression, but by then everything in my life had changed. I was no longer at home, with a well-stocked pantry open and available to me at all hours. I was in college, in a small town, where dinner was served from six to nine P.M. in the dining hall—period. There was one, and only one, alternative to campus food: D'Angelo's Pizzeria, which delivered up until midnight. But they only delivered to the dorm itself, not to the individual rooms. If you wanted to pick up your pizza, you had to go downstairs to the common room, which was always filled with other students studying or playing poker or watching TV.

I was six months into my freshman year when the next depression struck. It was the dead of winter. As an L.A. native, I'd never experienced a New England winter before, and I thought it was surely the end of the world. My body ached with lethargy. I could barely even move to shift positions in bed. The hypersomnolence returned in full force, even worse this time than before: now I was sleeping several days in a row. When I finally did awake, it was to the old familiar hunger, the unappeasable lust to bite and swallow and chew.

The campus dining hall was out of the question. I was incapable of taking a shower or washing my hair or even brushing my teeth, and there was no way I was going to allow myself to be seen like that. That ruled out ordering pizza, too. I couldn't risk being caught in the common room. So I stayed in my room, behind a locked door, only emerging in the middle of the night to go to the bathroom.

At one point, I went seven days in a row without any food.

By the eighth day, the pangs in my stomach were so intense I couldn't ignore them anymore. Late that night, when everyone else was asleep, I prowled the empty halls, searching for food. This soon became my nightly routine. I'd go from trash can to trash can, rifling through the contents as quickly as I could. Every once in a while I'd hit pay dirt: a discarded pizza box with one or two half-eaten slices remaining. I'd grab them and run as fast as I could back to my room, my haven, where I'd devour them in wolfish delight.

I was caught pawing through the trash on a couple of occasions by the night security guard, but I covered by saying that I was looking for my class notes, or a term paper, or something I had accidentally thrown out. As I saw it, I had no choice: I had to find food. My weight was dropping precipitously, and I was beginning to have severe dizzy spells. I was so fatigued it was all I could do just to drag myself from bin to bin to bin. Sometimes I was too weak even to hoist the lids. Finally, I passed out one night on the way back to my room. I woke the next morning in the infirmary, with a doctor at my side, shaking his head.

"We have to call her parents," he said to the nurse. I listened through the door: "Yes sir, it's treatable, but it's a pretty bad case. Severe malnutrition. We don't often see it up here at Vassar, but I did my residency in South Philly and I know all the signs."

The doctor walked over to me and held out the phone. "Do you want to speak to your father?" I shook my head and turned my face to the wall, forcing myself to focus on the large pastel poster that was hanging next to the window. To this day, I still can't see a Degas ballerina without instantly feeling a hot flood of shame.

There was no way I could explain my behavior to Daddy. He might understand about the strange eating habits—he had, after all, understood once before—but the root of those habits was beyond his comprehension. I knew, because I had already tried several times without success to tell him about the depression: "the black beast," as I called it back then. But Daddy was from the simple, straightforward Kansas plains. Metaphors only made him itch between the shoulder blades. "Just tell me what's wrong and we'll fix it" was his infuriating reply. What was wrong? Everything and nothing, all at the same time.

When I got out of the hospital, a few pounds plumper but no wiser, I went back to my scavenging. I had become addicted to the risk, the thrill. I became good at it, too. By my junior year, I could dig through an entire bin in two minutes flat. I could hear the guard coming long in advance, and scurry back to my room before he could even catch a glimpse of my shadow.

Which is why, much as I loved Vassar, I was relieved to see those four years end. I knew that I was graduating one swift step ahead of scandal. Law school, I thought, had to be better. At least I would have my own apartment, safe from prying eyes, and a car to get around in. And who knew? Maybe with the change of scenery my depressions would dissipate. Maybe I wouldn't even get depressed at all.

It was a lovely dream, which lasted all the way up to and halfway through my first contracts seminar. By the end of that class I knew that I had made a serious mistake. I should never have gone to law school. I was an English and art history major, for God's sake, not a right-wing, right-brain entrepreneurial type. Business bored me, and I lacked the proper reverence for money. So it was no great surprise that the black beast was waiting to greet me when I got home. The depression that descended upon me that first year of law school was unlike any I had previously known. It was as if all my past depressions were just training, leading up to this, the ultimate war.

As the darkness deepened, so did my hunger. It penetrated my bones to the marrow, a constant throbbing reminder of the emptiness inside. Although I knew there would never be enough food to satisfy my cravings, that didn't stop me from trying. I bought in bulk from wholesale grocery stores: sheet cakes and slabs of beef and cases of canned spaghetti. I ate it all in a rhythmic numbness. Whenever possible, I used my fingers instead of a fork. The food felt somehow more satisfying, less illusory that way. I ate until I fell asleep. Then I woke, and ate some more.

On the average, these episodes lasted five days. Every binge was followed by a week or two of remorse and self-recrimination. For the first time in my life, I was actually gaining weight. I was putting on as much as ten pounds per binge, and I didn't know what to do about it. My identity was tied up in a size six body—or better yet, a size four. Thin to me meant more than pretty. It meant disciplined, empowered, in control: all the attributes I secretly knew I lacked. But mostly, the illusion of a sound and healthy body was essential camouflage. I needed it to hide the evidence of an unsound mind.

This was well before bulimia became a household word. I'd heard of girls at Vassar shoving their fingers down their throats to lose weight in a hurry. I tried sticking my fingers down my throat, over and over and over again, with no success. I gagged, my face grew red and apoplectic, but the food would not come up. Finally, I decided it was time for drastic measures: I would fast the food away. Fasting was easier than dieting. Dieting required moderation, and my bipolar genes operate best in black and white, not gray.

Self-imposed starvation, I discovered, is different from hunger. It's subtly fueled by pride. "I've fasted eight days, why not make it ten," you soon begin to tell yourself. Ten becomes eleven, eleven quickly turns to fourteen. As weak as your body may be, your spirit is lifted by the knowledge that you have created this fast, this shining monument to self-denial, all on your own.

My hip bones were my guide. When they clearly protruded from my body, it was safe to start eating. But I remained vigilant, scrutinizing my naked body every day for hours at a time in the mirror until I lost all sense of a normal physique. I expected my belly to be not just flat but concave, and the slightest hint of a swelling would instantly start me fasting again. But no matter how strict I was with myself, no matter how thin I became, depression was always waiting for me, eager to undo all my discipline with its omnivorous hunger. Again and again I gained back all the weight I had lost. Then pound by pound, I would fast the weight away.

Binge/fast. Binge/fast. I was two distinct people: the one who showed herself in public but never ate, and the one who never saw the light of day and did nothing but eat. I even had different wardrobes for the different identities: chic designer clothes in bright, come-notice-me colors for the thin girl versus shapeless, billowing swaths of black for the fat one. I wore hats in both phases, but while the thin girl sported beribboned boaters and saucily tilted berets, the fat one stuffed her greasy hair beneath a baseball cap and prayed that no one would look at her. I lived this dual existence for a good twenty years, managing by stealth and luck never to be seen in my binge phase by anyone who mattered to me. I had a few close calls—curious boyfriends, mostly, pounding on the door and wondering where I was—but I never allowed anyone to get close enough to discover my secret.

I've always lived alone, by necessity, and I thought I always would. Then something miraculous happened. After years of trying one mood stabilizer after another, I finally discovered a medication that works. I wouldn't say that the black beast is banished altogether, but it's manageable. Whereas before I could expect to spend at least half of each month in the throes of depression, now whole seasons go by without my ever once contemplating suicide. Now when I suffer, it's usually for a damned good reason, one that has nothing to do with my dopamine or serotonin or norepinephrine levels. The guy didn't call when he said he would, maybe, or the car needs a brake job I just can't afford.

With my brain chemistry finally in some semblance of balance, you'd think that my body would soon follow suit. After all, I can't remember the last time I binged. With depression at bay, I just don't feel the need to anymore. But my body doesn't seem to care that I'm sane. Apparently it has a mind all its own, and food is still the enemy.

To ward off the inevitable pain and distension, I find myself eating less and less with each passing day. As a result, I've gradually wasted away, from a petite but relatively normal size four to a two to my current size zero. What's less than a zero I don't want to know. While obesity may be a national epidemic, you don't see people going up to perfect strangers to tell them that they are too fat. But apparently there is a social consensus that thinness is in the public domain. Rarely a week goes by without someone commenting on my body, telling me I need to "put some meat on those bones," or "have a cookie, for God's sake."

I do my best to avoid all reflective surfaces—mirrors, shop windows, shiny spoons, and the like. I tell myself, like a mantra, that genuine beauty is more than skin deep. But it's impossible to feel even remotely beautiful when strangers are constantly pointing out your flaws. Do they think that I haven't noticed myself? No doubt they assume that I'm anorexic, and can't see what's right in front of my eyes. They couldn't be more mistaken. I mourn my breasts, my hips, the former softness and roundness of my upper arms. I miss the swell of my buttocks against a tight pair of jeans, the subtle fleshy friction between my thighs. I long for some kind of cushioning against the sharp edges.

But mostly I long for sustenance—a sense of fullness, an absence of ache. It's a primal hunger, that goes beyond food:

what I really crave is normalcy. I want to sit down at dinner with another human being and do more than push the meal around the plate. I want to go to the movies and toss back popcorn, go to a ball game and gorge on hot dogs. I want to join the Friday night gang at Guido's for fried calamari and veal Milanese. I want to say yes, finally yes, to an oatmeal cookie.

So tomorrow at ten I'll see yet another in a long, long line of specialists. I'll let him poke and prod with his rubber-gloved fingers and cold metal instruments. I'll swallow the shame and tell him my story. "Why have you waited so long to seek treatment?" he will ask. Because I never thought life could be any different. I thought I would always be mentally ill, that depression owned me, body and soul. I never had a long enough glimpse of clear blue skies to believe in anything but bad weather. And now? It's simple. I'm hungry again.

16

I look harmless enough, I suppose. Sitting here
on this park bench, watching the nanny parade pass by, I
probably look like a quiet, tolerably well-groomed woman
in her early forties, who's just killing time. Waiting for an
appointment, perhaps, or maybe waiting for a rendezvous.
The waiting part is right. I am waiting; I have been waiting; I
do nothing but wait. And the killing part is right, too—except
it isn't time I want to kill, it's that chipper young nanny in the
gold velour sweats with the cherubic-faced child in her arms.

I was young once, too, if never chipper. But I did have
great expectations from life. After all, but for a recurring
mental illness, for a few years there I had it all: a good

education, a lover who desired me, a lucrative job. I call them "the Prozac years," that glorious span in my thirties when everything seemed to go my way. For the first time in my life, a medication was actually working. Prozac seemed to knock me out of depression, but it didn't kick me up into mania. Instead, it nudged me ever so subtly into hypomania, every manic-depressive's dream.

Hypomania is that idyllic interlude just before mania when all of your senses are in a state of heightened arousal. But they don't overwhelm you. Nothing overwhelms you. The sun never shines too bright, but you feel its warmth on your skin. The wind never blows your hair awry, but it whisks the clouds away. Life is liquid and even; it balances.

I met Alan when I was hypomanic. He was the kind of man no one ever thought to call "Al." He was the top rainmaker in our firm. I was a humble associate who had somehow managed to attract his notice. He told me later that it was a combination of things: an appellate brief I wrote, an outspoken comment I made at the annual firm picnic, and the way my red hair gleamed against a gold silk scarf. "You stood out" was all he said when I asked him why he chose me above all the rest of my peers to be on his team.

So I was on the inside at last, and I liked it fine. But with the overconfidence bred of hypomania, I knew that I could get inside deeper still if I focused all my energies on it. I started staying at work later every night, churning out memo after memo addressed to Alan's attention: crisp, well-researched, thoroughly gratuitous memos designed solely to make his life a little bit easier, and to focus a brief but shining spotlight on me.

It worked. I was finally called into Alan's office. He was, as always, impeccably dressed, in a single-breasted charcoal gray suit with thin pinstripes. His glowing white shirt had the signature French cuffs. It was his trademark, to shoot his cuffs just before the kill. I'd seen him do it in court and more frightening still, in the office, when he fired someone in my presence.

Alan was on the speaker phone. He motioned me to sit down without ever looking in my direction. Fifteen minutes later, he was still on the phone, and I was still sitting quietly. His conversation did not appear to be going well. Legalisms were shot through with four-letter words, culminating with Alan slamming down the receiver.

He looked up at me and grinned. "Well, that was fun," he said. "Fun?!" I asked. "That guy just called you a slimy son of a bitch." Alan laughed. "Yeah, but look who got the last word in. It gave the appearance of closure. And never forget: appearances matter."

He looked me slowly up and down. I knew that I had passed.

He then handed me a folder stamped "Privileged/ Confidential." It contained all his trial notes for the upcoming lawsuit that everyone was talking about, by far the hottest case in the office. We represented three major studios, and stood a good chance of getting the business of several more if we won. The stakes were high, and competition to get on this small but elite team was fierce.

"Read the file and we'll discuss it over dinner," Alan said. He didn't stop to ask if I already had plans. Nor did I expect him to. This was the inside, after all. The deep inside. What could possibly be more important than that?

At dinner, to my surprise, Alan didn't talk at all about the lawsuit. In fact, he talked about everything but: his childhood, his Princeton years, his current dreams and aspirations. We both consumed a fair amount of cabernet that evening, but I knew it wasn't the wine talking. It was the hypomania, working its magic. I had seen this before: normally reserved men breaking down or opening up or otherwise deactivating all their defenses in my presence.

I've looked in the mirror when I'm hypomanic and even I can see it: my eyes are an open invitation, a bottomless well of empathy. "Trust me, tell me everything," they say, and people do. Not just men sitting across from me at a candlelight dinner, either; and not just men, for that matter. Men and women everywhere seem compelled to talk to me, touch me, give me their confidence. It happens in the oddest places: in the aisles of the supermarket, waiting in a movie line, sitting at a coffeehouse, and *especially* in elevators. Hypomania breaks down that invisible wall that exists between well-mannered strangers. There are no strangers anymore, only unknown friends, waiting to tell me their stories.

When Alan walked me out to my car, he leaned against the fender and pulled me into his arms. He took his time. He didn't kiss me all at once—he nibbled, as if tasting me for flavor. Then he gradually, bit by bit, as if he had all the time in the world, explored my lips. It was the single most persuasive kiss I'd ever received in my life, doing justice to his reputation as the lawyer who could convince you of anything. By the end of that kiss, I was willing to go anywhere, do anything, feel whatever Alan desired.

This continued for the next couple of months. We worked together during the day without ever betraying our after-hours feelings. Then once or twice a week, we would have dinner, followed by a heavy-duty petting session in the parking lot. As the weather grew colder, we finally took the action inside. We went back to the office and made out like randy teenagers on Alan's couch (I was too junior to merit comfortable armchairs, let alone a whole couch). But always, just as we were on the verge of actually making love, Alan would stop, put his hand gently over my mouth, and say, "Wait. It isn't time yet."

Well, I knew a thing or two about time, and in my opinion, it was way overdue. This was as close as I had ever come to the absolute inside—a senior partner at one of the top firms in town, who was handsome and famous, and who knew how to kiss a girl silly. Plus I actually liked him. Our wry senses of humor played well off each other, and the quickness of his mind never failed to astonish me. I even swooned when he corrected my grammar. After every sweaty session on the office couch, I used to go home and fantasize about our future. It was just a matter of time, I figured. As long as I stayed hypomanic, anything was possible. I could even be one of those smiling young women I saw pushing their strollers through the park every Sunday afternoon. As long as I stayed hypomanic, I could have it all.

As the days of work grew longer and more intense, I became justifiably worried. I knew that lack of sleep is a primary trigger for mania. And indeed, I could feel myself getting more and more agitated with each successive sleepless night. But the biggest problem, of course, was Alan. Early on, in a fit of intimacy following an exceptionally head-spinning bout of kissing, I had told him that I was manic-depressive, but that it was under control. He held me at arm's length and stared at me with his cross-examination stare. "It had damn well better be, because I've got a lot riding on you," he said.

I knew what he meant. Neither of us mentioned it by name, but we were both thinking the same thing. A sexual harassment lawsuit was the last thing Alan needed at this juncture in his career. I kissed him as convincingly as I possibly could, and he allowed himself to be convinced. But the issue festered between us from that day forward, more powerful in its silence than it ever would have been if openly explored.

I hid my symptoms from Alan, and from everyone else, as best I could. Fortunately, every lawyer preparing for a major trial is snappish and irritable. My accelerated speech went unnoticed. We were all talking a mile a minute, troubleshooting rat-a-tat-tat like machine gunners under heavy fire. In short, we were wired, and none more so than Alan, who seemed to subsist solely on black coffee and M&Ms. In the midst of this, my own steady ascent into mania went largely unnoticed. Except by me. I knew damn well what was happening, and I begged my doctor to fix it before it got out of control. But all he could offer was the suggestion that I take a leave of absence to try out some new medication.

A leave of absence! After everything I'd been through to get where I was, did he honestly think I could just walk away? I knew that the second I stepped out the door, five other associates would be clawing one another's backs to take my place. So no, I told my doctor, leaving was not an option. He gave me a prescription for a new mood stabilizer. But first, he said, we'll have to wean you off the Prozac, which means that things may get much, much worse before they ever get better.

And sure enough, within forty-eight hours, I was walking and talking so fast even my own shadow couldn't keep up with me. Alan complimented me on the amount of work product I was generating. In fact, he was so impressed by my overall energy and drive, he even made me second chair on the trial, an unheard-of honor for an associate at my level. But like all of Alan's career decisions, it was a well-calculated move. I was an automaton at that point, at his beck and call twenty-four hours a day. I didn't sleep; I didn't eat; I just worked, in a single-minded frenzy. I was über-lawyer: not only efficient, but nasty to boot.

Needless to say, we won the trial. It was a big-time victory, covered by all the papers. "Tonight," Alan said, catching me alone in the hall and whirling me about, "we celebrate."

I knew what that meant—or at least I thought I knew. Surely tonight, it would finally be "time." What else could Alan be waiting for? That night, a dozen outfits later, I finally achieved the desired look: a simple black sheath with a Chanel chain-link belt and a long rope of pearls. It was elegant, which Alan liked, and deceptively demure, which he liked even better. Deceptive because underneath the basic black, I was anything but: I had on the fancy Paris lingerie that I'd never dared wear before. Lacy silver-snap garters, sheer silk stockings, and a black satin camisole. Like all the best lingerie, it left everything to the imagination and nothing to chance.

Alan's face lit up when he saw me, then he proceeded to ignore me for the rest of the meal. It wasn't his fault, really. People kept coming up to us every five minutes to congratulate him and talk about the case. I decided to concentrate on the plate in front of me instead. I couldn't remember when I had last stopped to eat, but all of a sudden I was ravenous, not so much for the food itself, but for the sensations: the tingle of champagne, the crunch of the baguette. Alan had ordered caviar, and every spoonful felt like tiny explosions against the roof of my mouth. Between the beluga and the garter tickling each thigh, I was halfway to orgasm and Alan hadn't even touched me yet—much less talked to me.

I finished off my champagne and signaled for another glass. Our waiter, Jarrod, was a dead ringer for Cary Grant, complete with English accent. He certainly had all the requisite charm, even complimenting me on my dress, which is more than Alan had found time to do. In between courses, we held a running conversation while Alan chatted up colleagues. I learned that he was (surprise, surprise) an actor, and that he was about to open in an Equity waiver production in Hollywood.

"You should come," Jarrod said. His hand briefly brushed against mine as he refilled my glass.

You have to understand what mania does to the skin: it lights up every nerve ending. The slightest sensation feels like a volcanic eruption—and there I was, swathed head to toe in silk, my flesh ripe with desire. And who was feeding me, pouring me wine, paying me attention? Not my date, but this gorgeous young man with the Cary Grant cleft in his chin.

Alan was still talking to the man at the next table. Bridges are only kindling, I thought. I decided to torch this one.

I waited until Alan was looking in my direction, reached in my purse and pulled out a card. Smiling sweetly, I asked, "Honey, do you have a pen? I want to give this guy my phone number." Alan shook his head, looking a bit bewildered, I thought. "Oh, never mind," I said. "I'll just use Jarrod's pencil." And I did, scribbling my digits on the back of the card and handing it to Jarrod with the most meaningful smile in my arsenal.

"In fact, Jarrod, what are you doing later tonight?" I asked, crossing my legs to expose a glimpse of garter. "Maybe we could have a drink after hours somewhere."

Alan was stunned. Jarrod looked at him and beat it, mumbling something about the crème brûlée.

"Just what do you think you're doing?" Alan demanded.

"Having fun," I said, sipping champagne.

He reached over and took the glass from my hand. "You're manic, aren't you?" he asked.

Never, but never, call a manic person "manic" to their face. For some reason, when you're in the very throes of it, the term *manic* sounds like the most degrading, insulting, offensive character slur imaginable. I suppose it's like accusing a drunk of being an alcoholic: beneath the accusation is the threat that you're going to take the drink away. So when Alan called me manic, I instinctively twisted away from him.

"How dare you," I hissed, and got up so abruptly that I knocked the champagne bucket over. It spilled onto the table and all over Alan's suit. I watched with satisfaction as the signature white cuffs grew piss yellow with wine. Then I turned and walked out of the restaurant.

He was right. I was manic. I knew it, but I couldn't think beyond the moment. All that mattered was how I looked in my own mind, making the grand exit.

It took me a whole week to calm down, a long, miserable week during which the mania finally peaked and then crashed, giving way to unimaginable despair. I thought I knew depression in all its many flavors and layers, but never had I known a depression like this.

After two weeks off work (during which I claimed, as always, to have the flu), I finally dragged myself into the office. All I wanted to do was clear off my desk and apologize to Alan, but he was away on vacation. And he wouldn't be back for another three weeks.

It took me only two to realize that what was wrong with me was deadly serious, more serious than anything I had suffered to date. It wasn't just depression. It was a suicidality so intense and profound that I had to throw away the steak knives and turn all my pills over to my therapist for safekeeping. My psychopharmacologist again told me that I had to take a leave of absence. This time, for the first time, I listened.

It was supposed to be a three-week leave. But three weeks stretched to six, then nine, and still I was no better. I didn't hear from Alan the whole time, and I certainly didn't call him. I didn't have the will or the energy to call anyone, let alone someone to whom I owed a serious apology. Plus, it seemed monumentally unfair somehow that I should have to apologize for the actions of someone I barely knew. Sure, I'd met that manic redhead before, the one who spilled the wine and walked away. We frequented the same mirror, I'd seen her in passing. But it's not like we were actually related. As far as I was concerned, she'd hijacked my flesh, and I shouldn't be held responsible for anything my body had done while she was in control of it.

It would have been a comforting philosophy, if I'd been capable of being comforted. But deep down I knew I was liable. Liable for everything I'd ever said and done to Alan, regardless of who was ruling my brain chemistry that day: the manic seductress or the anxious associate or the lovesick fool who sneaked daffodils onto his desk every Thursday. I knew how different each one was from the other, but it didn't matter. They were all someone the world knew as me.

I finally managed to pick up the phone late one Friday night, not because I was feeling any better, but because I had reached the last gasp of despair. Part of me didn't want to die. Not yet, not like this. I needed an infusion of hope, a reason why I should go on living. Who was the smartest man I knew? Surely Alan would have all the answers. If he didn't, then no one did.

To my surprise, Alan was home when I called him. He even sounded happy to hear from me and concerned to know how I'd been. "First let me apologize," I said, and a wave of relief swept over me when I was through. To my astonishment, taking responsibility for my manic misconduct didn't feel like an admission of guilt. It felt like an acceptance of my illness, in all its many facets. It felt like surrender. This is who I am, I thought: sometimes manic, sometimes depressed, but always and inescapably manic-depressive.

"Just give me one good reason," I said. "No, it doesn't even have to be a good one. Just any reason whatsoever why I should stay alive. You know me. Can you think of one?"

The line was silent. I knew better than to interrupt Alan when he was thinking. At least, I hoped he was thinking. I hoped he hadn't set the phone down and walked away in disgust. But no, I could hear his breathing—long, slow, steady breaths, which I assumed was a good sign. I shut my eyes and tried to match my breathing to his. It was the closest I'd felt to him in months.

"Okay, there's something you should probably know," Alan finally said, and to my surprise I thought I detected the slightest hint of a quiver in his voice.

"Yes?" I prompted, gently.

He cleared his throat and mastered the quiver. "I would marry you in a minute," he said, "if it wasn't for the manic depression."

I heard the word *marry*, and I heard the words *manic depression*, but my mind refused to combine them into a sentence. "I'm sorry, I think I misunderstood you. Could you say that again?" I asked.

"You heard me," he said.

"And *that's* your reason why I should stay alive?"

"That's one reason," he said. "I just thought you should know."

Call it cowardice, call it courage, call it whatever you will, but I kept silent until I felt I could speak without any overt anger. "Thank you, Alan, I'll think about that," I finally said, politely. "But it's time for me to take my medication now, so I'd better say good-bye."

"Good night," he said.

"Good-bye," I corrected, but I'm not sure he could tell the difference over the phone.

I lay down on my back and stared up at the ceiling and counted my dreams, one by one, as they vanished. Orange blossoms, bassinet, white picket fence: gone, gone, gone. "If it wasn't for your manic depression," he'd said. Well, if it wasn't for my manic depression, there would be no me for him to marry, period. I'd be some other person entirely. I wouldn't have those flashes of brilliance that he so admired, that made him want me in the first place. I wouldn't have the volatility that maddened but intrigued him. Alan hated ordinary. That's just what I would be.

Damn him for being so smart, and not smart enough to see this. I closed my eyes and let the anger radiate out to my fingertips. Depression had deadened me for such a long time, I'd forgotten what pure, unadulterated emotion felt like. I cared again; I cared deeply. I was on fire. I was furious. I was alive. So Alan did have the answer after all, it seemed, although his words had a far different impact than he probably intended. Rather than inspiring hope of any kind, they ignited such a rage in me that I vowed to stay alive, just to prove him wrong.

By the time I was finally able to return to work, I discovered that Alan had left the law firm for a lucrative in-house position at one of the major studios. I was crushed. Not because I missed him, the anger had cured me of that, but because Alan was still the salt in my wounds. I needed the sting of him to remind me that I had survived.

Eventually, with time and a new medication, the anger subsided, and my feelings for Alan faded. I forgot his birthday. I forgot his favorite film. I forgot everything about him, in fact, except the sound of his voice telling me "if it wasn't for the manic depression."

He was partly right, of course. Alan was always at least partly right. Every Sunday I sit on the same park bench, and I watch the inside pass me by. If it wasn't for the manic depression, I think . . . but no; I refuse to listen. There are other voices here, far more deserving. Across the park, a nanny in gold velour sweats pushes a child on the swings. Even from this far away, I can hear the child laugh.

17

"A lady doesn't scratch," my mother used to warn me, in her "company manners" voice. She never told me what a lady ought to do with her itches. Suppress them, I suppose. That's what ladies did with all their natural urges: they resisted the temptation to scratch.

Well, I was itchy all over, and not just my skin. I squirmed in the chair, trying to get comfortable, then Greg's cell phone rang again. Banning cigarettes in restaurants was a major step toward civility. Now we need to ban cell phones as well. But for once, I welcomed the rude distraction. While Greg was talking, I slid my hand under my napkin and scratched the length of my left inner thigh, back and forth, up and down, over and over until the itch finally subsided. By the time Greg hung up the phone, I was back to being a lady again, both hands neatly folded on top of the table, a polite smile poised at the edge of my lips. To look at me you would never guess that just beneath my pearls my heart was throbbing like a jackhammer. You would never smell the sweat. I was too sweetly perfumed.

But all afternoon, while I was dressing for this date, I had been so nervous I could barely function. Buttons refused to obey my trembling fingers. My mascara smudged, my lipstick smeared. This was torture. And yet this was, ironically, what I'd been hoping for most of my life: normal. For almost a year, I'd been on a medication that evened out the exaggerated highs and lows of my manic depression, that brought me as close to plain old sane as I'd ever been before. It was the longest stretch of sanity I'd known in twenty years. Perhaps that's why my fingers fumbled. It's hard to apply your makeup artfully when you barely recognize yourself in the mirror.

It was never this difficult to dress when I was manic. I just grabbed the sexiest jeans or the slinkiest dress and the highest pair of heels in my closet. Dressing was even easier when I was depressed. Nothing looked good on me, period. Nor did I ever expect it to. So I settled, inevitably, on basic black, which suited my pallor and mood. But how was I supposed to dress for normal? What message was I trying to send? I was hardly the manic vixen anymore, nor was I the graveyard ghoul. But both were ghosts inside me, and they chose my wardrobe. So I compromised, tossing out anything too ravishing or too repressed, because I was no longer a creature of extremes. This left me with very little to choose from, so little that I sat down on the bed, surrounded by piles of rejected clothes, and had myself a good cry. Who would have thought, after all these years of longing for it, that normal still meant feeling, and feeling doesn't always mean feeling good.

I went into the bathroom to wash my face. Could these be the lips that had kissed so many men? They looked like a child's lips now, pale pink and slightly puffy from crying—and yet there was a hint there, a something knowing in the corners. I looked down at my wrists. Three long white raised scars traversed the veins, relics of a dull, desperate razor. It seemed my body remembered my extravagant moods, no matter how hard my mind tried to forget them. But normal lived on inside my eyes. They shone with the remnants of a few stray tears, but they didn't blaze and snap like wildfire, nor were they as dull as sodden coals. They were simply eyes, looking back at me, wondering what next. As if I knew.

I heard my mother's soft, low voice: "You can always tell a lady by her pearls." I appraised my face, my normal eyes, my experienced lips. Yes, I could play a lady. I needed a role, I felt naked without one, and neither mania nor depression would do. So thank God I'd gone to Vassar: I knew how proper ladies should look and act. I knew what to do with my hands (keep them folded and quiet). I knew how to cross my legs (always at the ankle, then tilted slightly to the left). And I knew what to wear: pearls roped loosely at the neck, and a simple black dress with kind lines. My depression wardrobe was teeming with black dresses, so I picked the least severe of the bunch and tried it on with the pearls. At last, a costume that fit.

I was startled by the transformation. Not only my eyes but

my body looked somehow more capable, more at ease, as if they knew what to do next. I summoned up the memory of high tea in the Rose Room at Vassar: the beautiful, gracious women with their white gloves and witty remarks. I was one of them once. Perhaps I could be again.

But the Rose Room, with its quiet, faded elegance, its stiff damask linens and heirloom silver, seemed a long, long way away from the hip, buzzing restaurant that Greg had taken me to. The bar was packed with gorgeous young women in whispers of black, and older, slightly paunchy men with predator eyes. The tables were placed so close to one another that you had no choice but to eavesdrop, to the extent you could hear at all. It's practically impossible to hold a meaningful, intimate conversation at the top of your lungs. And then there was the cell phone, ringing every five minutes, snapping any thread of conversation I managed to get going.

Maybe it was for the best, I thought, when Greg's phone rang again. I didn't know what to say, anyway. While I scratched my inner left thigh, I wondered why I was still so ill at ease with this man. He was, without a doubt, the most ambivalent man I'd ever dated. He liked me intermittently, in between his other women. I never knew when he would call, or not call, or want to see me, or ignore me altogether. He was a "player," and the worst thing was, I knew it and I still hung around. When he was present, it was worth it. He was kind and generous and charming, so much so that occasionally somehow seemed better than never at all. And I didn't really want commitment, anyway. Just a little consistency.

But his ambivalence fired up my competitive streak and

made me long for his attention even more. What did he want? Over the course of the past few months I had tried on role after role—pal, seductress, mother—but none of them seemed to make any difference. Tonight, I tried on lady. I knew that Greg had a snobbish side to him, so there might be some appeal. But watching his eyes rove hungrily over the lithe young bodies at the bar, I could tell it wasn't working.

The situation felt hopeless. But there was a way out, a surefire solution just within my reach: the wine list. I'm really not supposed to drink. Alcohol destabilizes me instantly, plus it interacts adversely with every one of my drugs. But just because it's so forbidden to me, it was suddenly all that I desired.

The table to my immediate left had just ordered after-dinner drinks, and they were so close I could smell the bite of brandy in the air. I watched them swirl their glasses while they talked. When they drank, I closed my eyes and swallowed, too, trying to conjure up the feel of liquid fire down my throat. I remembered brandy. I remembered vodka, too. Salt still tasted like tequila sometimes, summer still smelled like vermouth.

Alcohol was alchemy, instant mood magic. Whatever I was feeling at that moment, I knew that I could feel different, and soon, with just a few sips. More likely than not, I would start to get manic, and then at last the words would come, more words than I possibly knew what to do with, more words than could ever fit into my mouth. The ease would come, too, the blessed nonchalance. Because when I'm manic, I may think you are fascinating, but I don't particularly care what you think of me. I already know that I'm fabulous.

But what a wonderful time we would have together, for

those first few sips, at least. Then there's no telling which way my mood might go. I might soar to the ceiling, giddy with laughter, drunk on my charms. Or I might just suddenly deflate and collapse right in front of you, a soggy heap overflowing with tears. Either way, I'll demand another drink.

I looked over at Greg, chatting on his cell phone, oblivious to the time bomb that was ticking away right across the table from him. I thought to myself, it will serve him right for ignoring me. He'll have a hard time pretending I don't exist after a couple of drinks. I'll be so incredibly charming, maybe he'll forget about all those other women for a while. As if in a trance, I watched my hand steal of its own accord past the dinner plate, over the menu and around the salt shaker to the wine list. "I'll just study it to kill time while he's on the phone," I thought, although I noticed that my fingers were trembling a bit as I turned the first page.

Then I forgot everything: Greg, the swirling snifters, the other women at the bar. I was thoroughly absorbed, and by such fascinating characters: Perrier Jouët, Dom Pérignon, Châteaux Margaux. I knew all of them so well, their traits, their subtle idiosyncrasies. I knew the legends of their births. I knew them better, in a way, than I knew Greg.

"Did you see something you like?" Greg's voice cut in on my reverie. "Well, there's a magnificent Margaux," I started to say, then caught myself. "But I'm not drinking tonight, so I'm sure you don't want to order a whole bottle." I put the wine list back in its place and folded my hands in front of me.

"You can just have a sip," Greg said, and signaled to the waiter.

"No, really, I don't want to drink tonight," I said, but the waiter was already at Greg's side taking his order, the fabulous Margaux. Then Greg's cell phone rang again, and at least he apologized profusely this time before taking the call.

Within minutes, the bottle was at our table and Greg had nodded his approval of the label and the waiter was removing the cork and starting to pour. I started to tell him that I didn't want any, but Greg put his hand over the phone and said, "Just have a sip." And by then the glass was half-full. And calling my name.

I was distracted for a moment by a sudden commotion at the bar. One of the long-legged blondes had spilled a drink all over herself, and apparently found it hilarious. Her laughter rang out over the general din, attracting the attention of all the men around her, several of whom were eagerly patting her body with napkins. "I wish I could be that oblivious to what people think of me," I thought to myself. But the jealousy only lasted an instant. I knew that I could. The difference between a lady and a tramp, in my case, was probably no greater than a few glasses of wine.

I picked up the glass by the bowl and held it up to the light. It was a classic Margaux, deep ruby red with purple undertones. When the light struck it just right it almost glowed scarlet. The last time my wrist had been this close to that particular shade of red, it had been swimming in its own blood. The warm bathwater had glowed scarlet too, for a time. That was over six years ago, and I hadn't tried to harm myself since. Nor had I had a drink in all that time. I was more than just sober now. I was verging on sane. And for all of my qualms about normal—what to wear or how to behave—the truth was, I actually liked being sane.

I liked waking up in the morning knowing that more likely than not, I would probably meet all my commitments that day. I wouldn't have to cancel, to come up with excuses, to weather disapproval and sidestep shame. I would remember everything I had done the night before, and it would probably be boring and a trifle routine. After so many years of not knowing what fresh hell was next, how I adored boring and a trifle routine.

At that moment, Greg set his phone down and turned back toward me. "Sorry about that," he said. Then he picked up his glass. "To us," he said, and I froze. Greg had never been the least bit romantic before, never come close to suggesting that "we" might ever be "us." How was I not supposed to drink to that? And yet I knew that there would be no we, no us, no me anymore if I did. Greg would find himself sitting alone with a stranger, someone he had never met before and definitely never invited to dinner. She might be terrifically entertaining at first, might even rival the blonde at the bar in brazen allure, but after that, who knew? All that was certain was that however much fun she had tonight, I would be the one to wake up with the hangover and all the bitter memories. Or worse yet, with no memories at all.

So with infinite care I brought the glass halfway to my lips, then let the stem slowly slide all the way through my fingers, an inch at a time until the tiniest sliver remained in contact with my skin. Then I let go. The glass dropped to the table and shattered. Wine instantly engulfed the white tablecloth, spreading between me and Greg, a bright bloody red.

Greg didn't embarrass or accuse me, he simply called the waiter over to change the linens. "And bring her another glass," he said. This time I spoke up loudly enough for him—for the whole restaurant, no doubt—to hear. "Thank you, but no," I insisted, and the "no" suddenly echoed in one of those odd, quick interludes of silence that occasionally descend on a noisy crowd. I didn't mind. I was rather proud of that no. It deserved to be heard. It may have sounded like no to a glass of wine, but in truth it was no to a great many things. And yes to a great many more.

18

The valet sprang into action the second my car pulled up to the curb. He opened the door and extended his hand to help me out, unfurling a sleek gray umbrella and complimenting me on my shoes, all at the same time.

"Pretty hot," he said. "Ferragamo or Blahnik?"

"Right," I replied, a bit flustered, trying to find my footing on the wet pavement. I wondered if he was expecting a tip. But you weren't supposed to tip at private parties, were you? It had been years since I'd been to a big Hollywood bash, and I didn't know what to expect from anyone or anything that evening, especially myself.

I covered my confusion by giving the valet the sexiest

smile I could manage. He seemed satisfied, abandoning his post to escort me up the long, slippery cobblestone path to the front door. I was extremely grateful for his steady grip on my elbow, grateful just to have a man, any man, at my side while I approached the buzzing crowd ahead.

Two uniformed guards stood on each side of the door. I had been invited to the party only the night before, so there had been no time to deliver my invitation, the proof of my legitimacy. I was pretty sure that I wasn't on the list. It was up to me and my sassy shoes to convince the guards, the other guests, and most of all myself that I belonged there.

If only I had a date beside me. . . .

The umbrella became redundant once we reached the covered porch, as did the valet, unfortunately. I thanked him as sweetly as I could, braving the awkward moment of tipless leave-taking with a bright, stupid smile. Watching him walk away in those snug rented pants, I felt a brief but violent urge to run after him and throw myself on his mercy. But I was trapped in the crowd's surge toward the door, where a guard waited, hand outstretched.

"Invitation?" he said.

"I'm sorry," I said. "I don't actually have one. You see—"

"Name?"

I gave it. He flipped through the list. The crowd behind me was getting impatient. I could feel their collective irritation burning a hole in my back, straight through my shoulder blades to the guard's stubby little fingers, which were still rifling through the pages. He straightened up and spoke to the empty air above my head.

"Not on the list," he said. "Next."

If you haven't worn high heels in a really long time, they can make you awfully cranky. So it wasn't entirely my fault that my voice had a decidedly peevish edge to it when I finally snapped to and remembered my training.

"Look here," I said. "I'm with the host. I'm a lawyer. I'm his lawyer, in fact, and he was expecting me an hour ago. I know he won't be happy that you've kept him waiting this long."

"But you're not on the—" he started to protest. I cut him short.

"Of course I'm not on the guest list. This is business, not pleasure." I opened my purse and started to poke around in it. "I'm sure you've heard of the law offices of . . ." I combined several names from several different well-known firms. "I've got a card in here somewhere."

"But your name's not—"

I clicked my purse shut. The lawyer approach clearly wasn't working. It was time to shift gears, and fast. "Give me a break, okay? My feet are killing me in these shoes."

I lifted my left foot and rubbed it slowly up and down my right ankle. He shook his head, grinned, and waved me through. Just in time, because the truth was I didn't have any cards of any kind in my purse. Since this was technically a date, not business, I had assumed that lipstick, a comb, and breath mints would come in far handier than proof of my J.D. But I'd forgotten one of the cardinal rules of Hollywood: Never confuse beauty with credibility.

I used to be deadly credible. I reveled in the quick changes of expression my business card would elicit, from surprise to respect to a tinge of fear, depending on the person's past experience with lawyers. But always, no matter what, the card made a difference. I may not have been the prettiest girl at the party, but people, especially men, took me seriously.

So what the hell was I going to do now, with only a MAC sheer plum lipstick to my name, if someone asked me about myself? I looked around the room. In every direction, I was surrounded by drop-dead beautiful women. I smoothed my own dress: a relic from my past, but until now reliable. I looked classic, perhaps even chic in the right lighting and as long as my zipper stayed shut. But my dress wasn't going to be doing the talking for me. If I stayed, I was going to have to talk, to flirt, to charm, to cajole. In other words, to party.

Damn my new medication. Just when I most needed the brazen, spitfire sociability of mania, I was stable. Stable and sane and oh so very boring in comparison. Just like my dress.

A waiter passed by with a tray of drinks. Alcohol is one of the surest, quickest ways I know to precipitate a dangerous upswing in my mood. Two martinis and I'm in manic wonderland, going on about the virtues of the olive and the lore of vermouth and any other subject that catches my fancy to a spellbound audience that gradually thins out as the oration wears on. But while my thoughts may have lunged at the passing tray, my body stayed put in stability, too slow and too sane to chase after a fleeting whim.

It was definitely time to move on. I wasn't manic enough to compete with a room full of models. It's a measure of my insanity that I sometimes think I am.

I pushed my way through the heavy cleavage to the foot of

the staircase, then up to the first floor. I tiptoed to the nearest door, which opened onto a magnificent master bath: spotless, sterile, and mine, all mine. I pulled the door shut behind me and locked it.

I was wearing my Swiss watch that night, the tiny gold one with multiple functions, including a little alarm I use for my medications. I carefully set it for ten minutes, then emptied my purse onto the counter and faced the mirror. Ten minutes all alone with the cool Carrara marble, or at least until someone came knocking. Ten minutes to splash cold water on the back of my neck and figure out what on earth I would possibly say if someone asked me what I did for a living, which was bound to happen eventually.

"I'm sick for a living" didn't quite sound right. "I live on federal disability" was true enough but no better. I could always just say I'm a lawyer. That was true, too, but highly misleading. I still have a valid professional license, but I rarely practice law anymore. Manic depression makes it too easy for me to screw up, and I'm terrified of screwing up. I worked too many years at too many big firms, where mistakes are considered mortal sins and you could go to hell for a typo.

I snapped open my compact and leaned in closer toward the mirror. I have no illusions about my abilities when my meds aren't working. When I'm manic, I think every case is a surefire winner, and every client a potential lover. So I never practice when I'm manic, if I can help it. I also don't practice when I'm depressed. I simply can't. I'm brain-dead from the neck up, and the rest of me is paralyzed, overwhelmed by the sheer effort of blinking.

When, on occasion, a job presents itself during saner, more competent times, I jump for it. I almost always win. And so I almost always wonder, everyone around me wonders, why I can't just keep on practicing long enough to make a decent living? Just enough so I wouldn't have to pray each night for food and rent for one more month, please God, just one more month. But always, after I've aced that final deadline, a reaction sets in: sometimes mania, sometimes depression, frequently suicidal. Nothing, not even a pitcher of martinis, can destabilize me so completely.

It took me sixteen years to realize this. Sixteen years of reassuring myself on the way to work every morning that there's no such thing as a happy lawyer. It was just this particular case I was working on, this client, this judge, the latest Supreme Court ruling, the airborne viruses in my corner office. Perhaps if I tried another firm. So I tried another firm, several other firms in fact, each one bigger and better and more prestigious than the last. I landed higher-profile clients and took long, exotic vacations, and made a considerable amount of money. And I went to parties, a whole lot of parties, for every cause imaginable, or no cause at all. I billed the time regardless.

It was all about client development then. Every warm, sincere handshake, every sweet "tell me more" represented another tenth of a billable hour to me. I never squandered my smiles. So I wasn't in the least bit lying back then when I whipped out my card and announced "I'm a lawyer." That's what I was. That's all I was.

If you nurture it long enough, a lie can become a life. Bad nights don't surprise you much after sixteen years. You come to expect them. You just don't expect them to go on forever. I should have known that the bout of depression that finally ended my career was the worst one yet, when I ran out of business cards and didn't have the energy to order new ones. Nothing mattered to me at that point except the pain, and the pain was everywhere. No matter how hard I tried to hide it behind crisp suits and careful makeup, it showed in my face and body. Strangers kept asking me if I was sick. I couldn't fool anyone, not the senior partners or the clients or the court, or most of all, myself.

I took a lengthy leave of absence, and then I left for good. Gradually, I was dropped from the mailing lists: the artsy invites, the special passes, the comp tickets slowed to a trickle. Eventually, they were replaced entirely by bills.

It was just as well, I told myself. All my clothes were outdated anyway. But the real problem wasn't that I had nothing to wear. It was that I had nothing to say. Being an attorney had made me very unhappy. But not being an attorney made me invisible, in my eyes at least. My whole adult identity had vanished, along with the money and trappings that had so clearly defined my prior existence. In their place was a formless, shapeless, terrifying blob: the nonbillable hour. How was I supposed to fill it? Would it never end?

As if on cue, my watch alarm went off and I jumped, practically toppling off my high heels. Ten whole minutes gone, and all I'd accomplished was to chew off my lipstick and revive the worry lines between my eyebrows. And damned if there weren't traces of tears in the corners of my eyes, threatening my mascara. Tears for what? I didn't miss the life. But God, how I sometimes missed the lie.

A little magic with the mascara wand, a fresh slick of lipstick and a spritz of perfume, and I looked like a new woman. I spun around, watching my skirt whip nicely around my thighs. There wasn't a hint of inappropriate curve to my hips when I turned and looked sideways in the mirror. Everything was where it should be, for a change. Everything except me. I looked at my watch. Five more minutes gone. I had to get out of this bathroom.

I gathered up the items I had dumped out onto the counter: lipstick, comb, mascara, compact, and stuffed them back into my little purse. There would even have been room for a couple of business cards in there. Why on earth didn't I take any with me? I knew the answer, even though I found it hard to believe. The card was a lie, a false front, and I was sick to death of lies. I was stable, the medication was working. What was wrong with reality? I had a choice, I realized. I could go downstairs and simply tell the truth about who I was and what I did. I knelt down on the bath mat and said a quick prayer: "Dear God, please let me tell the truth and please let it be okay." And with that, I went downstairs.

The party had grown while I was shut away in the bathroom. People lined the staircase, overflowing onto the landing. I was only a few steps away from the bathroom when I heard someone call my name. It was the host. "Where have you been?" he shouted. "I've been looking all over for you. Here, I want you to meet some people."

He introduced me to six or seven strangers and asked me if I wanted a drink. "Mineral water, please," I said, sticking with stable, and then I turned back to his guests.

"You look familiar," said the man on my right. "What do you do?" There it was: first question, first encounter.

"You look really familiar, too," I said, stalling. "Where could we have met?"

"I own a gallery on La Brea," he said. "Do you collect?"

"I used to," I said. "Back when I was a . . ." "Lawyer" was on my tongue. I improvised. "Lover. An art lover. I really used to love art." A hot flush crept over my cheeks, and I dropped my eyes. This was harder than I thought. Fortunately, the host came back at that moment with my drink, and started talking about a mutual friend. When he left, the gallery owner returned to the same question.

"Sorry about that," he said. "So tell me again—what do you do?"

I took a deep breath. "I'm manic-depressive," I said. "And I'm writing a book about my experience."

"Excuse me? I didn't quite hear you."

I repeated it loudly, emphasizing the words *manic-depressive*. I was suddenly the center of the circle's attention, with a half dozen pairs of eyes turned toward me.

No one spoke for several seconds. Then a tall man across the circle said, "My therapist thinks I might be manic-depressive. How can you tell?" I started to answer, but the woman next to him interrupted: "My mother's bipolar. They just found out, and put her on lithium. She's, like, normal for the first time in her life. Is it true it's genetic?"

I nodded, but before I could speak the gallery owner put his hand on my arm and said, "You know, I could tell just by looking at you that you were going to be interesting. Wasn't

Van Gogh bipolar, too?" The tall man said, "Yeah, but Byron is the ultimate manic-depressive. That's why my therapist thinks I might be. He says I'm Byron-esque." The pride in his voice would have been touching if it weren't so silly. But I held back my laughter, because questions were now peppering me from all sides: What's it feel like to be manic? Do you have visions? Could I get manic if I tried? and so forth. I answered what clinical questions I could about the best friend, the boss, the stepson, the lover. Of the seven people in the circle, five of them had some connection to the disease, and they all craved information.

By the time I sneaked a peak at my watch, twenty minutes had gone by and my mouth was bone dry. I tried to excuse myself from the conversation, but a handsome Latino in a tuxedo, a newcomer to the circle, stopped me. "I hear you're manic-depressive," he said. "So's my sister. But she's not half as pretty as you." He raised my hand to his lips and actually kissed it.

What the hell was going on here?

I decided to make a break for the bathroom, which was still empty. Not much had changed in the last thirty minutes. If anything, I looked a little worse for the wear. My hair needed smoothing, my nose was slightly shiny, and my lips had lost their artificial luster. So why were tall tuxedoed strangers beaming at me and kissing my hand? Why was I surrounded by eager, interested eyes? I took a quick inner inventory. No, I wasn't manic. I wasn't imagining the attention, either. I could still feel the warmth of it on my skin. The why of it was a mystery, though.

Up until the gallery owner, no one had paid much

attention to me. Even he had initially been merely polite, with that old "you look familiar" opening line—until he asked what I did for a living, and I told him the truth. That was it, the point where polite had turned into deeply personal. No wonder the men were attracted. When those words *I'm manic-depressive* came out of my mouth, suddenly I was wearing the most revealing outfit in the room. The other women may have had plunging necklines and slits clear up to their waists, but I was standing there without any armor at all.

I couldn't wait to get back to the party and tell them everything. I ran a quick comb through my hair, touched up my lipstick, and powdered my nose—then forced myself to sit back down on the tub and count to one hundred. Eagerness is good for the complexion, but it's a tad too close to mania for my comfort. I took several deep, even breaths, still counting. Maybe I could tell them about the time I was manic and almost got arrested for speeding but seduced the motorcycle cop instead. Or the time that I tried to kill myself and got rescued by my exterminator. Or the night that I . . . no.

No, no, no.

This was precisely the reason I make myself stand very still when the urge to move is strongest upon me. By the time I had finished counting to one hundred, I realized that telling the truth is a dance like any other, with steps and rhythm and etiquette. It had taken me a lifetime to learn how to lie. I would have to devote a little more time to studying the art of disclosure. So I closed my eyes and simply listened: to my breath, to my blood, to the light patter of the last remaining raindrops on the roof, to the faint snatches of Ella Fitzgerald seeping through the walls. I listened for answers. When none were forthcoming, I realized that listening itself was the answer for now.

I was ready. I stood up, stretched, and walked out of the bathroom without even a sideways glance in the mirror. I'd had enough of my own reflection for one evening. Besides, I very much wanted to dance.

Epilogue

I'm sitting in my favorite café, writing a line,

crossing it out. Writing a line, crossing it out. My soft-boiled

egg will be cold by the time I get around to cracking its shell.

My latte will have lost all its foam. I don't care. I've had

the best meals of my life here in this little café, writing and

crossing it out.

The waiters know by now not to disturb me. I sit for hours

(I tip really well), hunting for just the right word, the right

rhythm to express what I hear inside my head. Some days I

never find it. The man at the next table laughs too loudly.

Dishes rattle in the kitchen. A woman walks by on her way to

the bathroom, her stilettos clicking. I tear the page off my legal pad, and crumple it up in disgust. But I don't despair. Even at my most discouraged, I don't despair.

For this day, at least, I'm sane, and I'm writing, and that's a glorious thing.

It's all you can really count on when you're manic-depressive: this day, and no more. But the days add up. To my surprise, it's been several years since I've had a full-blown manic episode, longer still since I've tried to commit suicide. Stability feels like such a precarious thing, dependent on just the right dose by just the right doctor. But still, somehow I've found it—at least long enough to spend another afternoon in the little café.

Life is not easy, but it's simpler now. I no longer want to fly kites in a thunderstorm. I have no interest in dancing a tango with the riptide. I can leave my best friend's boyfriend alone. But I would like to see Santa Fe again. This time in summer, I think.

Los Angeles, California
April 18, 2007

Acknowledgments

In the midst of madness, I've encountered extraordinary kindness. My deepest thanks and love go out to the following people:

To Geoffry White, the only true humanitarian I've ever met, who has saved my life so many times I'm afraid I've stopped counting. Without him, this book would still be a dream.

To the wise and generous Nancy Bacal, my writing teacher for God knows how many years. She made me dig deeper than I ever thought possible, then taught me how to recognize buried treasure.

To the intrepid pilot Bob Young, who fed me through a straw when I was too ill to eat, then ferried me around town when I couldn't drive. He's seen me at my worst, and stayed the course. Words can never repay my debt.

To my dear friend, the talented hunk Paul Mantee, whose

wicked way with laughter and women is camouflage for a squishy heart.

To my champion, the warm and wonderful Lisa Doctor, whose enthusiasm for my book was contagious. Her heart knows no bounds.

To Linzi Glass, whose gift with words is exceeded only by her talent for friendship.

To Arnold Pomerantz, who is a constant reminder that goodness does exist in this world.

To the brilliant and loyal Larry Downes, who believed in me early on.

To Phil Green of Autonomy Entertainment, who took a chance when he didn't have to.

To Steve Brourman, who interrupted his whirlwind life long enough to give me back my dignity.

To Juliet Green, who always spoke the truth.

To all the gifted, quirky, and compassionate characters in Nancy Bacal's Wednesday-afternoon and Monday-night writing groups, past and present. With special thanks to Maureen Miller, James Fearnley, Kim Kowsky, Ann Bailey, and Janet Tamaro.

To John Wolff, who put up with more than his fair share, and to whom I'll always be grateful.

To my lovely and indefatigable agent, Lydia Wills at Paradigm, who cared about every word. May she never see another gratuitous semicolon again.

To my gentle but incisive editor, Sarah Durand, who nudged me into a better book when all the odds were against it.

To Dr. Harvey Sternbach, Dr. Jeff Davis, Dr. Rita Resnick, Suzy Davis, Terry Hoffman, Karen Lorre, Kathy Jackoway, David Seligman, Chris Blake, Emily Krump, Sherrill Martin, and Elizabeth Suti for their wisdom and encouragement.

To my beautiful and courageous mother, who has lived through everything I've written about and then some, and loved me nonetheless.

And to my father, for everything.

A Discussion with Terri Cheney

Following the success of Manic, *readers and reviewers around the country had many questions for Terri Cheney. We've collected a random sampling of some of those questions with answers from Terri, but if you need any additional information, you can contact Terri through her Web site, www.terricheney.com.*

1) *Manic* **was a bestseller in hardcover, reaching tens of thousands of readers. How do you feel about so many people being privy to the intimate details of your private life that you kept hidden for so long? Has this changed your life in any way?**

My secrets were weighing so heavily on me by the time I wrote *Manic* that it felt tremendously liberating to get them out in the open. But I have to admit it's unsettling whenever I meet someone whose first line is, "I've read your book." That person already knows infinitely more about me than I'll probably ever know about him. He knows, for example, that I was raped, that I spent a night in jail, and, of course, that I'm bipolar. Small talk seems pointless after that.

One of the benefits I've discovered from disclosure is that strangers now tell me their secrets. Because I've been forthcoming about my own struggle with mental illness, they trust me to listen to their stories—the wild ups and downs, the desperate consequences, the hassles with the health-care system, the constant fear of stigma. Discovering that my secrets weren't so extraordinary after all is a gift I never expected.

2) *Manic* is told in such an untraditional manner—it's not a linear narrative at all—so many of the characters' lives aren't wrapped up nicely and neatly. Can you tell me a little more about some of the players in your life and what they're doing now? What about your mother? Your former boyfriends?

My mother is alive and well. It was hard for her to read some of the darker passages in *Manic*, which she didn't know about, but she's inordinately proud of me—she carries around some of my press clippings, at all times. Perhaps because she's a registered nurse, she is able to understand that bipolar disorder is a physical disease, and she accepts it.

I still remain friends with most of the boyfriends I wrote about in *Manic*, except Alan, the man who said he'd marry me in a minute if it weren't for my manic depression. We've lost touch, which may be for the best. But Jeff and I are very close, and he's been one of my biggest cheerleaders. And to my great surprise, Rick—the man I thought I'd never, ever see again after punching him in the jaw during a mixed state episode—showed up at one of my readings. We've been able to discuss the past and make peace with it, which I never thought would happen.

3) With a topic as personal as mental health, you've probably received letters from readers who relate to your struggles. What responses have you received from readers? How has the public's reception of the book affected you? Have there been any reactions that you weren't expecting?

Before *Manic* came out, I worried about how the public's response would affect me and whether it would exacerbate my illness. I am highly sensitive to criticism, as I think many people with bipolar disorder are, but overall, the response to my book has been very positive and very heartfelt. Of course, now and then I've received a negative response or review, a few of which have been surprisingly severe (one man wrote that he wished I would have succeeded at my suicide attempts), but with my therapist's help, I've usually been able to place the negativity in perspective. Any subject as loaded as mental illness is bound to evoke strong responses.

4) I'd like to talk a little about what you're doing now and what the future holds. How do you manage your manic depression now? Did the writing of this book help your treatment in any way?

I haven't had a manic episode in well over six years—and no, I don't miss it, as many people ask. Mania got me in too much trouble. I do still get depressed, but the depressions are much less frequent and intense, and to my amazement, I don't get suicidal. The basics of my recovery regime are: medication (which is often tweaked), therapy, support groups, mental health advocacy, and writing. I have excellent relationships with my therapist and psychopharmacologist, two amazing men. My weekly groups include the dual diagnosis group that I facilitate at UCLA for people with mental illness and substance abuse issues and my two writing groups, which provide invaluable emotional support.

Writing for me has always been cathartic and therapeutic. People often ask, "Wasn't it traumatic to describe the events in *Manic*?" No. To the contrary, it was empowering to revisit some of the most dismal times of my life and cast them in prose. They no longer owned me after that.

5)   What advice would you give to someone who's either struggling with manic depression or has a friend or loved one who is?

For people with manic depression, the fear of stigma can be crippling—preventing them from getting help and having the necessary compassion for themselves. For these people, I'd like to emphasize that bipolar disorder is first and foremost a physical disease. You wouldn't hesitate to treat a broken leg; why neglect a broken mind?

Another critical lesson I wish I'd learned sooner is that sobriety is essential to sanity. Many manic-depressives in the throes of the disease self-medicate, and I can understand why, but the prescribed medications simply don't work if you do. There are numerous support groups available through the resources section of my Web site, www.terricheney.com, to help you attain the sobriety that can change the course of your disease.

As for family and friends, I think you have to take care of yourself first so you have something left to give to others. I highly recommend NAMI (the National Alliance on Mental Illness, www.nami.org), a family-based organization that understands the special difficulties of dealing with bipolar loved ones.

6) What are you working on now?

One of the things that surprised me most about the e-mails I received was how many of them were from parents of bipolar children. Their passion and persistence, their unrelenting dedication to finding help and educating themselves, simply amazed me. There are clearly more bipolar children out there than I ever realized, and there is a critical need for greater awareness.

So I've decided to write a childhood memoir about growing up bipolar. I don't think I had a typical childhood (who did?), and I believe one of the reasons for that was the illness. Few "normal" children are suicidal at seven, for example. I hope that writing this book will help me make peace with my chaotic childhood, the same way *Manic* helped me lay my more recent ghosts to rest.

Signs and Symptoms of
Mania and Depression

Millions of people around the country either suffer from manic depression or have a friend or loved one who does. While Manic eloquently describes the roller-coaster ride of one woman's life, the symptoms may not be so clear for others. In Terri Cheney's own words, here are some of the symptoms, and their aftereffects, that one might suffer.

DEPRESSION

Paralysis: Movement is impossible, so I typically stay in bed for days, getting up only to crawl to the bathroom.

Excessive sleep: I sleep for three to four days straight.

Excessive eating: When I'm not sleeping, I'm eating. I often gain up to ten pounds during a depressive episode.

Desire for isolation: I spent a good part of my career as a lawyer hiding out under my desk.

Extreme negativity: When I'm depressed, I think mania's a myth. I can never remember feeling any other way. I'm convinced that I always have been, and always will be, doomed to depression.

Suicidal tendencies: Before I was properly medicated, I tried to kill myself numerous times, resulting in several hospitalizations. At the time, given the severity of my depressions, suicide seemed like the only sane option.

MANIA

Increased energy: During manic episodes, I can zip through all the work I couldn't touch while I was depressed.

Sexual impulsivity: I've been known to pick up the waiter right in front of my dinner date.

Heightened sensuality: My nerve endings snap alive when I'm manic. I can taste colors; I can smell sounds.

Grandiose thinking: One night when I was driving home I decided to challenge the cypress tree in front of my house to a battle of wills. I was sure I was the stronger force and could make it move out of my way. I wasn't, and my car was totaled.

Decreased need for sleep: I often go up to four days without the ability to, or the desire for, sleep.

Decreased need for food: When I'm manic, food is just a distraction that keeps me from talking or doing other "really important things."

Excessive spending: I went through my entire savings during one glorious spree at the Post Ranch Inn.

Irritability: Nothing—nothing!—moves fast enough for me when I'm manic.

Recklessness: I danced naked in a freezing riptide for hours one night without any concern that I was putting my life in peril.

Charisma: The upside of mania is that people seem inexplicably drawn to you.

Recommended Reading

An Unquiet Mind: A Memoir of Moods and Madness by Kay Redfield Jamison

Touched with Fire: Manic-Depressive Illness and the Artistic Temperament by Kay Redfield Jamison

The Bipolar Child: The Definitive and Reassuring Guide to Childhood's Most Misunderstood Disorder, Third Edition by Demitri Papolos, M.D., and Janice Papolos

Bipolar Disorder for Dummies by Candida Fink and Joe Kraynak

Living Well with Depression and Bipolar Disorder: What Your Doctor Doesn't Tell You . . . That You Need to Know by John McManamy

Loving Someone with Bipolar Disorder by Julie A. Fast and John D. Preston

Electroboy: A Memoir of Mania by Andy Behrman

Surviving Manic Depression: A Manual on Bipolar Disorder for Patients, Families, and Providers by E. Fuller Torrey and Michael B. Knable

The Bipolar Disorder Survival Guide: What You and Your Family Need to Know by David J. Miklowitz

Internet Resources

National Alliance on Mental Illness: www.nami.org
An excellent family-based organization, especially useful for loved ones seeking information and support. This is the primary source I recommend to the public.

Depression and Bipolar Support Alliance: www.dbsalliance.org
Free information on depression and bipolar disorder, as well as listings to over one thousand patient support groups across the country.

National Institute of Mental Health: www.nimh.nih.gov

Electroboy.com: www.electroboy.com
Sponsored by Andy Behrman, author of Electroboy: A Memoir of Mania.

About.com: Bipolar Disorder: bipolar.about.com

Dual Recovery Anonymous: http://draonline.org
A twelve-step approach to dual diagnosis—mental illness combined with substance abuse, a serious problem that affects a great number of bipolar persons. Includes educational material as well as listings of local support groups.

Child and Adolescent Bipolar Foundation: www.bpkids.org
Focuses on problems of parents and kids with pediatric bipolar disorder. General information for the public, as well as an online professional directory for members.

Bipolar Child: www.bipolarchild.com
Sponsored by Demitri Papolos and Janice Papolos, authors of the bestseller The Bipolar Child. *Provides a model IEP plan, bipolar questionnaire, and an excellent newsletter re cutting-edge pediatric issues.*